THIS WORKBOOK BELONGS TO:

_____

STUDENT WORKBOOK
THE GREAT GATSBY

Use this workbook to get the most out of your reading.
Answer questions completely and thoughtfully.

COPYRIGHT INFORMATION

This is copyrighted material.

The purchaser may copy the student materials
for his or her classroom use only.
It may not be copied or distributed for any other purpose
without written permission from the publisher.

No portion may be posted on the Internet
without written permission from the publisher.

Copyright violations are prosecuted to the fullest extent of the law
and are subject to a minimum of a $500.00 fine,
imposed by the publisher
in addition to any other legal judgments obtained.

ISBN 978-1-60249-503-6
Copyright 2014
All Rights Reserved

Table Of Contents

Chapters 1-2
    Reading Activity 1: True or False? 7
    Reading Activity 2: Analyzing Passages 10
    Reading Activity 3: Physical Attributes & Characterization 13
    Reading Activity 4: Action, Character, Decision 14
    Reading Activity 5: Figurative Language 15
    Reading Activity 6: Elements of Fiction & Literary Devices 17
    Reading Activity 7: Meaning And Inferences 19
    Writing Activity 1: How Do Men Relate To One Another? 21
    Writing Assignments 23
    Quick-Write Assignments 24

Chapter 3
    Reading Activity 1: True or False? 27
    Reading Activity 2: Analyzing Passages 30
    Reading Activity 3: Minor Characters 33
    Reading Activity 4: Action, Character, Decision 34
    Reading Activity 5: Figurative Language 35
    Reading Activity 6: Elements of Fiction & Literary Devices 37
    Reading Activity 7: Meaning And Inferences 38
    Writing Activity 1: Who Is Gatsby? 41
    Writing Assignments 43
    Quick-Write Assignments 44

Chapters 4-5
    Reading Activity 1: True or False? 47
    Reading Activity 2: Analyzing Passages 50
    Reading Activity 3: Foil Character Study 53
    Reading Activity 4: Action, Character, Decision 54
    Reading Activity 5: Figurative Language 55
    Reading Activity 6: Elements of Fiction & Literary Devices 57
    Reading Activity 7: Meaning And Inferences 58
    Writing Activity 1: How Is Social Class Depicted? 61
    Writing Assignments 63
    Quick-Write Assignments 64

Chapters 6-7
    Reading Activity 1: True or False? 67
    Reading Activity 2: Analyzing Passages 70
    Reading Activity 3: Static and Dynamic Characters 73
    Reading Activity 4: Action, Character, Decision 74
    Reading Activity 5: Figurative Language 75
    Reading Activity 6: Elements of Fiction & Literary Devices 77
    Reading Activity 7: Meaning And Inferences 79
    Writing Activity 1: Moral Failure In The Great Gatsby 82
    Writing Assignments 84
    Quick-Write Assignments 85

Table Of Contents, Continued

Chapters 8-9
- Reading Activity 1: True or False? 89
- Reading Activity 2: Analyzing Passages 92
- Reading Activity 3: Direct and Indirect Characterization 95
- Reading Activity 4: Action, Character, Decision 96
- Reading Activity 5: Figurative Language 97
- Reading Activity 6: Elements of Fiction & Literary Devices 98
- Reading Activity 7: Meaning And Inferences 100
- Writing Activity 1: Is Nick A Reliable Narrator? 103
- Writing Assignments 105
- Quick-Write Assignments 106

Overview
- Reading Activity 1: True or False? 109
- Reading Activity 2: Analyzing Passages 112
- Reading Activity 3: Character Culpability 115
- Reading Activity 4: Action, Character, Decision 116
- Reading Activity 5: Figurative Language 117
- Reading Activity 6: Elements of Fiction & Literary Devices 118
- Reading Activity 7: Meaning And Inferences 120
- Writing Activity 1: How Is The Great Gatsby A Tragedy, and What Lessons Are To Be Learned? 125
- Writing Assignments 129
- Quick-Write Assignments 130

MATERIALS: CHAPTERS 1-2
THE GREAT GATSBY

Reading Activity 1: True or False

Reading Activity 2: Analyzing Passages

Reading Activity 3: Physical Attributes & Characterization

Reading Activity 4: Action, Character, Decision

Reading Activity 5: Figurative Language

Reading Activity 6: Elements of Fiction & Literary Devices

Reading Activity 7: Meaning and Inferences

Writing Activity 1: How Do Men Relate To One Another

Suggested Writing Assignments

Quick-Write Assignments

NOTES
THE GREAT GATSBY

The Great Gatsby Chapters 1-2: True or False?

Write *True* or *False* in the blank next to each statement. Below the statement, explain why you chose true or false, referencing the text to support your choices.

_____ 1. Daisy is aware that Tom is having an extramarital affair.

_____ 2. Daisy will not divorce Tom because she is Catholic.

_____ 3. Nick believes that it is acceptable to look down on the working class.

_____ 4. Tom treats George with respect.

The Great Gatsby Chapters 1-2 True or False? Page 2

_____ 5. Myrtle is an elegant and sophisticated woman.

_____ 6. Nick leaves the party and goes directly home.

The Great Gatsby Chapters 1-2 True or False? Evaluation

List Your Group's Members: Your Group's Question # _____

_____   _____   _____

_____   _____   _____

1 = No, Not At All   **2** = A Little   **3** = Some   **4** = Yes   **5** = Yes, Very Well

Evaluation of Question # ___
Does the explanation support the answer of true or false?   1 2 3 4 5
Is there good textual evidence to support the answer?   1 2 3 4 5
Is the answer clearly stated?   1 2 3 4 5
                          Total Score _____ of a possible 15 points

Evaluation of Question # ___
Does the explanation support the answer of true or false?   1 2 3 4 5
Is there good textual evidence to support the answer?   1 2 3 4 5
Is the answer clearly stated?   1 2 3 4 5
                          Total Score _____ of a possible 15 points

Evaluation of Question # ___
Does the explanation support the answer of true or false?   1 2 3 4 5
Is there good textual evidence to support the answer?   1 2 3 4 5
Is the answer clearly stated?   1 2 3 4 5
                          Total Score _____ of a possible 15 points

Evaluation of Question # ___
Does the explanation support the answer of true or false?   1 2 3 4 5
Is there good textual evidence to support the answer?   1 2 3 4 5
Is the answer clearly stated?   1 2 3 4 5
                          Total Score _____ of a possible 15 points

Evaluation of Question # ___
Does the explanation support the answer of true or false?   1 2 3 4 5
Is there good textual evidence to support the answer?   1 2 3 4 5
Is the answer clearly stated?   1 2 3 4 5
                          Total Score _____ of a possible 15 points

The Great Gatsby Chapters 1-2 Analyzing Passages

Answer the questions following the quotations completely.

1. "Only Gatsby, the man who gives his name to this book, was exempt from my reaction — Gatsby, who represented everything for which I have an unaffected scorn. If personality is an unbroken series of successful gestures, then there was something gorgeous about him, some heightened sensitivity to the promises of life, as if he were related to one of those intricate machines that register earthquakes ten thousand miles away."

   What does the reference to the book suggest?

2. "When I came back from the East last autumn I felt that I wanted the world to be in uniform and at a sort of moral attention forever; I wanted no more riotous excursions with privileged glimpses into the human heart."

   What words are in conflict within the passage? What does this—and what the speaker yearns for—suggest about the speaker?

3. "But I didn't call to him, for he gave a sudden intimation that he was content to be alone — he stretched out his arms toward the dark water in a curious way, and, far as I was from him, I could have sworn he was trembling. Involuntarily I glanced seaward — and distinguished nothing except a single green light, minute and far away, that might have been the end of a dock. When I looked once more for Gatsby he had vanished, and I was alone again in the unquiet darkness."

   The word "alone" is repeated here; why is that significant?

The Great Gatsby Chapters 1-2 Analyzing Passages Page 2

4. "Miss Baker and I exchanged a short glance consciously devoid of meaning. I was about to speak when she sat up alertly and said 'Sh!' in a warning voice. A subdued impassioned murmur was audible in the room beyond, and Miss Baker leaned forward unashamed, trying to hear. The murmur trembled on the verge of coherence, sank down, mounted excitedly, and then ceased altogether."

   Instead of the words that Daisy is saying, the narrator instead describes the sound with words like "murmur," "tremble," "verge," "sank," and "ceased." What does this indicate about the conversation? About Daisy?

5. "Well, she was less than an hour old and Tom was God knows where. I woke up out of the ether with an utterly abandoned feeling, and asked the nurse right away if it was a boy or a girl. She told me it was a girl, and so I turned my head away and wept. 'All right,' I said, 'I'm glad it's a girl. And I hope she'll be a fool — that's the best thing a girl can be in this world, a beautiful little fool."

   What does Daisy mean by "fool?" How does that relate to the first part of the passage?

6. "Mrs. Wilson had changed her costume some time before, and was now attired in an elaborate afternoon dress of cream-colored chiffon, which gave out a continual rustle as she swept about the room. With the influence of the dress her personality had also undergone a change. The intense vitality that had been so remarkable in the garage was converted into impressive hauteur. Her laughter, her gestures, her assertions became more violently affected moment by moment, and as she expanded the room grew smaller around her, until she seemed to be revolving on a noisy, creaking pivot through the smoky air."

   How does the narrator's view of Myrtle change?

The Great Gatsby Chapters 1-2 Analyzing Passages Page 3

7. "'I told that boy about the ice.'" Myrtle raised her eyebrows in despair at the shiftlessness of the lower orders. 'These people! You have to keep after them all the time.'"

   Why is this ironic? What does it reveal about Myrtle?

8. "The only *crazy* I was was when I married him. I knew right away I made a mistake. He borrowed somebody's best suit to get married in, and never even told me about it, and the man came after it one day when he was out. 'Oh, is that your suit?' I said. 'This is the first I ever heard about it.' But I gave it to him and then I lay down and cried to beat the band all afternoon."

   What is Myrtle suggesting about the basis for her marriage? How might it relate to her willingness to have an affair?

The Great Gatsby Chapters 1-2
Reading Activity 3 Physical Attributes and Characterization

From the list of characters below, select three. Locate details about these characters' physical appearance in chapters 1 and 2. Complete the chart below using this evidence from the text. Then, after reviewing the quotes you selected, write about how these physical attributes form a clearer characterization. Use your books to locate significant details about each character's physical appearance (body, mannerisms, gestures, clothing, etc.).

Daisy | Jordan | Tom | George | Myrtle

Character	Quote 1	Quote 2	Quote 3	How do quotes inform characterization?

The Great Gatsby Chapters 1-2: Action, Character, Decision

Write **A** (for Action) **C** (for Character) or **D** (for Decision) in the blank next to each to identify whether the passage/statement advances the action, tells us more about a character, or provokes a decision. On the lines under each question, provide a short explanation of your choice.

____ 1. Reserving judgments is a matter of infinite hope. I am still a little afraid of missing something if I forget that, as my father snobbishly suggested, and I snobbishly repeat, a sense of the fundamental decencies is parceled out unequally at birth.

____ 2. "Gatsby?" demanded Daisy. "What Gatsby?"

____ 3. "Civilization's going to pieces," broke out Tom violently. "I've gotten to be a terrible pessimist about things. Have you read 'The Rise of the Colored Empires' by this man Goddard?".

____ 4. The bottle of whiskey — a second one — was now in constant demand by all present, excepting Catherine, who "felt just as good on nothing at all."

____ 5. Daisy! Daisy! Daisy!" shouted Mrs. Wilson. "I'll say it whenever I want to! Daisy! Dai —"

The Great Gatsby Chapters 1-2: Figurative Language

On the short line provided, write **F** for figurative or **L** for literal. On the lines under each question, explain how the botanical reference or imagery helps create meaning.

___ 1. And so with the sunshine and the great bursts of leaves growing on the trees, just as things grow in fast movies, I had that familiar conviction that life was beginning over again with the summer.

___ 2. The lawn started at the beach and ran toward the front door for a quarter of a mile, jumping over sun-dials and brick walks and burning gardens — finally when it reached the house drifting up the side in bright vines as though from the momentum of its run.

___ 3. Turning me around by one arm, he moved a broad flat hand along the front vista, including in its sweep a sunken Italian garden, a half-acre of deep, pungent roses, and a snub-nosed motor-boat that bumped the tide offshore.

___ 4. We walked through a high hallway into a bright rosy-colored space, fragilely bound into the house by French windows at either end.

___ 5. The whole town is desolate. All the cars have the left rear wheel painted black as a mourning wreath, and there's a persistent wail all night along the north shore."

___ 6. Inside, the crimson room bloomed with light.

___ 7. But we heard it," insisted Daisy, surprising me by opening up again in a flower-like way. "We heard it from three people, so it must be true."

The Great Gatsby Chapters 1-2 Figurative Language Page 2

_____ 8. "I love to see you at my table, Nick. You remind me of a — of a rose, an absolute rose. Doesn't he?" She turned to Miss Baker for confirmation: "An absolute rose?"
This was untrue. I am not even faintly like a rose. She was only extemporizing, but a stirring warmth flowed from her, as if her heart was trying to come out to you concealed in one of those breathless, thrilling words.

_____ 9. The lamp-light, bright on his boots and dull on the autumn-leaf yellow of her hair, glinted along the paper as she turned a page with a flutter of slender muscles in her arms.

_____ 10. The late afternoon sky bloomed in the window for a moment like the blue honey of the Mediterranean — then the shrill voice of Mrs. McKee called me back into the room.

The Great Gatsby Chapters 1-2: Elements of Fiction & Literary Devices

1. "When I came back from the East last autumn I felt that I wanted the world to be in uniform and at a sort of moral attention forever; I wanted no more riotous excursions with privileged glimpses into the human heart."

   What is "the East" associated with here?

2. "My family have been prominent, well-to-do people in this Middle Western city for three generations. The Carraways are something of a clan, and we have a tradition that we're descended from the Dukes of Buccleuch, but the actual founder of my line was my grandfather's brother, who came here in fifty-one, sent a substitute to the Civil War, and started the wholesale hardware business that my father carries on to-day."

   What qualities do the Carraways of the "Middle West" have?

3. "It was lonely for a day or so until one morning some man, more recently arrived than I, stopped me on the road.
'How do you get to West Egg village?' he asked helplessly.
I told him. And as I walked on I was lonely no longer. I was a guide, a pathfinder, an original settler. He had casually conferred on me the freedom of the neighborhood."

   How does Nick's relationship to setting change? Why is that significant?

4. Instead of being the warm center of the world, the Middle West now seemed like the ragged edge of the universe — so I decided to go East and learn the bond business. Everybody I knew was in the bond business, so I supposed it could support one more single man. All my aunts and uncles talked it over as if they were choosing a prep school for me, and finally said, "Why — ye — es," with very grave, hesitant faces. Father agreed to finance me for a year, and after various delays I came East, permanently, I thought, in the spring of twenty-two."

The Great Gatsby Chapters 1-2 Elements of Fiction & Literary Devices Page 2

What associations does Nick have with "the East"?

5. "It was a matter of chance that I should have rented a house in one of the strangest communities in North America. It was on that slender riotous island which extends itself due east of New York — and where there are, among other natural curiosities, two unusual formations of land. Twenty miles from the city a pair of enormous eggs, identical in contour and separated only by a courtesy bay, jut out into the most domesticated body of salt water in the Western hemisphere, the great wet barnyard of Long Island Sound. They are not perfect ovals — like the egg in the Columbus story, they are both crushed flat at the contact end — but their physical resemblance must be a source of perpetual confusion to the gulls that fly overhead. To the wingless a more arresting phenomenon is their dissimilarity in every particular except shape and size."

   What are the physical qualities of the land—what contradiction does Nick point out?

6. "I lived at West Egg, the – well, the least fashionable of the two, though this is a most superficial tag to express the bizarre and not a little sinister contrast between them. My house was at the very tip of the egg, only fifty yards from the Sound, and squeezed between two huge places that rented for twelve or fifteen thousand a season. The one on my right was a colossal affair by any standard … My own house was an eyesore, but it was a small eyesore, and it had been overlooked, so I had a view of the water, a partial view of my neighbor's lawn, and the consoling proximity of millionaires—all for eighty dollars a month."

   What is the difference between the two "Eggs," according to Nick?

7. "When they do get married," continued Catherine, "they're going West to live for a while until it blows over."

   What is associated with the "West" in the passage?

The Great Gatsby Chapters 1-2: Meaning & Inferences 1

Read the passages and answer the related questions.

1. *No — Gatsby turned out all right at the end; it is what preyed on Gatsby, what foul dust floated in the wake of his dreams that temporarily closed out my interest in the abortive sorrows and short-winded elations of men.*
    According to Nick, what caused him to become introverted?

2. *Her husband, among various physical accomplishments, had been one of the most powerful ends that ever played football at New Haven — a national figure in a way, one of those men who reach such an acute limited excellence at twenty-one that everything afterward savors of anti-climax. His family were enormously wealthy — even in college his freedom with money was a matter for reproach — but now he'd left Chicago and come East in a fashion that rather took your breath away: for instance, he'd brought down a string of polo ponies from Lake Forest. It was hard to realize that a man in my own generation was wealthy enough to do that.*
    What is Nick's impression of Tom?

3. *For a moment the last sunshine fell with romantic affection upon her glowing face; her voice compelled me forward breathlessly as I listened — then the glow faded, each light deserting her with lingering regret, like children leaving a pleasant street at dusk.*
    What does this description suggest about Daisy's state?

4. *So Tom Buchanan and his girl and I went up together to New York — or not quite together, for Mrs. Wilson sat discreetly in another car. Tom deferred that much to the sensibilities of those East Eggers who might be on the train.*
    What does this suggest about Tom?

5. *We went on, cutting back again over the Park toward the West Hundreds. At 158th Street the cab stopped at one slice in a long white cake of apartment-houses. Throwing a regal homecoming glance around the neighborhood, Mrs. Wilson gathered up her dog and her other purchases, and went haughtily in.*
    What does this passage reveal about Myrtle?

The Great Gatsby Chapters 1-2: Meaning & Inferences 2

Read the passage and answer the related questions.

About half way between West Egg and New York the motor road hastily joins the railroad and runs beside it for a quarter of a mile, so as to shrink away from a certain desolate area of land. This is a valley of ashes — a fantastic farm where ashes grow like wheat into ridges and hills and grotesque gardens; where ashes take the forms of houses and chimneys and rising smoke and, finally, with a transcendent effort, of men who move dimly and already crumbling through the powdery air. Occasionally a line of gray cars crawls along an invisible track, gives out a ghastly creak, and comes to rest, and immediately the ash-gray men swarm up with leaden spades and stir up an impenetrable cloud, which screens their obscure operations from your sight. But above the gray land and the spasms of bleak dust which drift endlessly over it, you perceive, after a moment, the eyes of Doctor T. J. Eckleburg. The eyes of Doctor T. J. Eckleburg are blue and gigantic — their irises are one yard high. They look out of no face, but, instead, from a pair of enormous yellow spectacles which pass over a nonexistent nose. Evidently some wild wag of an oculist set them there to fatten his practice in the borough of Queens, and then sank down himself into eternal blindness, or forgot them and moved away. But his eyes, dimmed a little by many paintless days, under sun and rain, brood on over the solemn dumping ground.

1. What is the significance of the use of the word "farm?" Why is it ironic?

2. What color are the men? Why is this significant?

3. Who is T.J. Eckleburg? What, according to the narrator, was the purpose of the billboard? Why is that significant, given its location?

4. Why is the position of the billboard's "eyes" significant?

5. What does the valley of ashes look like? What does it represent?

The Great Gatsby Chapters 1-2: How Do Men Relate to One Another?

In chapters 1-2, masculinity as a concept is explored primarily through Tom, and to a lesser extent Nick, as well as some minor characters.

The ways in which characters interact fuel a narrative by advancing conflict and therefore plot. *The Great Gatsby* is very much a novel about masculine identity and its prerogatives. This is apparent in how men interact with one another.

Using textual evidence from chapters 1-2, look for patterns to begin formulating an answer to the question "How do men relate to one another?". As you develop an answer, consider why it is significant. What do these relationship dynamics reveal about the characters? How do they create meaning in the novel?

To determine an idea about how men relate to one another:

1. Identify passages and quotes where Nick and Tom interact with other male characters.

2. Examine the context of your quotes.

3. Consider the connotation and denotation of key phrases in your quotes.

    a. What is the tone—friendly, adversarial, angry, competitive?
    b. Is there a conflict?
    c. What attitudes are the characters revealing or concealing in their language?

4. Look for patterns in your evidence. Is a word or idea repeated? Use these patterns to shape an answer to the question.

The Great Gatsby Chapters 1-2: How Do Men Relate to One Another?

Complete the chart to analyze information to develop ideas to write your essay.

Character	Quote/passage interacting with Nick	Quote/passage interacting with Tom	Observations
Tom		N/A	
Nick	N/A		
Wilson			
Dog Seller			
McKee			

The Great Gatsby Chapters 1-2: Creative Analytical Writing Assignments

1. Write a business plan by George Wilson for improving his gas station business, including how he would like to sell used cars and cater to more upscale clientele.

2. Write a flashback to when Daisy and Jordan first met and became friends.

3. Write a letter from Nick to his father, sent while Nick was a soldier in World War I.

4. Write a "solemn and obvious" editorial by Nick for the *Yale News*.

5. Choose a section of text from the dinner party scene in chapter 1 and write a meta-narrative of what a character is really thinking.

6. Write a love letter from Myrtle to Tom.

7. Write a paragraph describing what T.J. Eckleburg "sees."

8. Imagine that Jordan Baker keeps a diary. Write an entry that describes her first encounter with Nick.

9. Write scene with dialogue where Tom apologizes to Myrtle for striking her.

10. An ellipsis is a form of punctuation that signifies omission. At the end of chapter 2, locate the sentence: "…I was standing beside his bed and he was sitting up…" Write a paragraph describing what you imagine occurred (and Fitzgerald omitted) just before that sentence begins.

The Great Gatsby Chapters 1-2: Quick-Write Writing Assignments

1. Does Nick find Jordan attractive? What about her interests him?

2. How has being a soldier in World War I affected Nick?

3. Does Daisy overreact to receiving phone calls from Tom's "woman in New York"?

4. Does Gatsby have a mystical or magical quality to him? Describe it.

5. Is Nick a trustworthy narrator?

6. Nick claims that he reserves judgment of other people. Whether he does or not, in what ways could the characters be judged?

7. Why the emphasis on sports (football, polo) around Tom? What does this reveal about his character?

8. Is the gathering at Tom and Myrtle's apartment fun at all? If so, how? If not, why not?

9. Most of the characters in the novel are materialistic and obsessed with stuff. Which character seems most obsessed with things?

10. What is the novel suggesting so far about marriage? Is it a sacred bond?

MATERIALS: CHAPTER 3
THE GREAT GATSBY

Reading Activity 1: True or False

Reading Activity 2: Analyzing Passages

Reading Activity 3: Minor Characters

Reading Activity 4: Action, Character, Decision

Reading Activity 5: Figurative Language

Reading Activity 6: Elements of Fiction & Literary Devices

Reading Activity 7: Meaning and Inferences

Writing Activity 1: Who Is Gatsby?

Suggested Writing Assignments

Quick-Write Assignments

NOTES
THE GREAT GATSBY

The Great Gatsby Chapter 3: True or False?

Write *True* or *False* in the blank next to each statement. Below the statement, explain why you chose true or false, referencing the text to support your choices.

_____ 1. Gatsby is famous in New York because of the lavish parties he throws each weekend.

_____ 2. Gatsby and Nick are both veterans of World War II.

_____ 3. Nick claims that he is a dishonest person.

_____ 4. Nick drinks a lot at Gatsby's party.

The Great Gatsby Chapter 3 True or False? Page 2

_____ 5. Nick is in love with Jordan Baker.

_____ 6. Jordan prefers simpler, unobservant men as suitors.

The Great Gatsby Chapter 3 True or False? Evaluation

List Your Group's Members: Your Group's Question # _____

_____   _____   _____

_____   _____   _____

1 = No, Not At All **2** = A Little **3** = Some **4** = Yes **5** = Yes, Very Well

Evaluation of Question # ___
Does the explanation support the answer of true or false?   1 2 3 4 5
Is there good textual evidence to support the answer?   1 2 3 4 5
Is the answer clearly stated?   1 2 3 4 5
                            Total Score _____ of a possible 15 points

Evaluation of Question # ___
Does the explanation support the answer of true or false?   1 2 3 4 5
Is there good textual evidence to support the answer?   1 2 3 4 5
Is the answer clearly stated?   1 2 3 4 5
                            Total Score _____ of a possible 15 points

Evaluation of Question # ___
Does the explanation support the answer of true or false?   1 2 3 4 5
Is there good textual evidence to support the answer?   1 2 3 4 5
Is the answer clearly stated?   1 2 3 4 5
                            Total Score _____ of a possible 15 points

Evaluation of Question # ___
Does the explanation support the answer of true or false?   1 2 3 4 5
Is there good textual evidence to support the answer?   1 2 3 4 5
Is the answer clearly stated?   1 2 3 4 5
                            Total Score _____ of a possible 15 points

Evaluation of Question # ___
Does the explanation support the answer of true or false?   1 2 3 4 5
Is there good textual evidence to support the answer?   1 2 3 4 5
Is the answer clearly stated?   1 2 3 4 5
                            Total Score _____ of a possible 15 points

The Great Gatsby Chapter 3 Analyzing Passages

Answer the questions following the quotations completely.

1. "[Jordan's] gray, sun-strained eyes stared straight ahead, but she had deliberately shifted our relations, and for a moment I thought I loved her. But I am slow-thinking and full of interior rules that act as brakes on my desires, and I knew that first I had to get myself definitely out of that tangle back home. I'd been writing letters once a week and signing them: 'Love, Nick,' and all I could think of was how, when that certain girl played tennis, a faint mustache of perspiration appeared on her upper lip. Nevertheless there was a vague understanding that had to be tactfully broken off before I was free."

   What is Nick's "interior rule" here that "act[s] as brakes"?

2. "'See!' he cried triumphantly. 'It's a bona-fide piece of printed matter. It fooled me. This fella's a regular Belasco. It's a triumph. What thoroughness! What realism! Knew when to stop, too - didn't cut the pages. But what do you want? What do you expect?'"

   What does owning this possession say about Gatsby?

3. "I like to come," Lucille said. "I never care what I do, so I always have a good time. When I was here last I tore my gown on a chair, and he asked me my name and address – inside of a week I got a package from Croirier's with a new evening gown in it."

   "Did you keep it?" asked Jordan.

   "Sure I did. I was going to wear it tonight, but it was too big in the bust and had to be altered. It was gas blue with lavender beads. Two hundred and sixty-five dollars."

   What does the speaker's attitude toward her dress signify?

The Great Gatsby Chapter 3 Analyzing Passages   Page 2

4. "He smiled understandingly—much more than understandingly. It was one of those rare smiles with a quality of eternal reassurance in it, that you may come across four or five times in life. It faced—or seemed to face—the whole external world for an instant, and then concentrated on you with an irresistible prejudice in your favor. It understood you just as far as you wanted to be understood, believed in you as you would like to believe in yourself, and assured you that it had precisely the impression of you that, at your best, you hoped to convey."

Why the repetition of "understandingly"—what does the word mean in this context?

5. "It made no difference to me. Dishonesty in a woman is a thing you never blame deeply – I was casually sorry, and then I forgot. It was on that same house party that we had a curious conversation about driving a car. It started because she passed so close to some workmen that our fender flicked a button on one man's coat."

What does this attitude reveal about Nick?

6. "'But how did it happen? Did you run into the wall?' 'Don't ask me,' said Owl Eyes, washing his hands of the whole matter. 'I know very little about driving — next to nothing. It happened, and that's all I know.'

'Well, if you're a poor driver you oughtn't to try driving at night.'

'But I wasn't even trying,' he explained indignantly, 'I wasn't even trying.'"

How is the word "indignantly" significant here?

The Great Gatsby Chapter 3 Analyzing Passages Page 3

7. "Every one suspects himself of at least one of the cardinal virtues, and this is mine: I am one of the few honest people that I have ever known."

   Why is the word "suspects" significant?

8. "' At the enchanted metropolitan twilight I felt a haunting loneliness sometimes, and felt it in others – poor young clerks who loitered in front of windows waiting until it was time for a solitary restaurant dinner – young clerks in the dusk, wasting the most poignant moments of night and life."

   What is the effect of the city on Nick and others like him?

The Great Gatsby Chapter 3 Reading Activity 3: Minor Characters

Complete the chart below using relevant quotes from the text that show how minor characters comported themselves at Gatsby's party. Then, after reviewing the quotes you selected, make observations about how the characters' behaviors reveal cultural mores (habits, manners, norms) of the times.

Character	Quote 1	Quote 2	Quote 3	Observations about cultural mores
Jordan's date				
Girls in yellow				
Owl Eyes				

The Great Gatsby Chapter 3: Action, Character, Decision

Write **A** (for Action) **C** (for Character) or **D** (for Decision) in the blank next to each to identify whether the passage/statement advances the action, tells us more about a character, or provokes a decision. On the lines under each question, provide a short explanation of your choice.

____ 1. I was on my way to get roaring drunk from sheer embarrassment when Jordan Baker came out of the house and stood at the head of the marble steps, leaning a little backward and looking with contemptuous interest down into the garden.

____ 2. It was testimony to the romantic speculation he inspired that there were whispers about him from those who found little that it was necessary to whisper about in this world.

____ 3. We talked for a moment about some wet, gray little villages in France. Evidently he lived in this vicinity, for he told me that he had just bought a hydroplane, and was going to try it out in the morning.

____ 4. I wondered if the fact that he was not drinking helped to set him off from his guests, for it seemed to me that he grew more correct as the fraternal hilarity increased.

____ 5. But I am slow-thinking and full of interior rules that act as brakes on my desires, and I knew that first I had to get myself definitely out of that tangle back home.

The Great Gatsby Chapter 3: Figurative Language

On the short line provided, write S for simile, M for metaphor or N for neither. On the lines under each question, explain how the use of figurative language creates meaning.

___ 1. In his blue gardens men and girls came and went like moths among the whisperings and the champagne and the stars.

___ 2. By seven o'clock the orchestra has arrived, no thin five-piece affair, but a whole pitful of oboes and trombones and saxophones and viols and cornets and piccolos, and low and high drums.

___ 3. At least once a fortnight a corps of caterers came down with several hundred feet of canvas and enough colored lights to make a Christmas tree of Gatsby's enormous garden.

___ 4. A humorous suggestion was made that she sing the notes on her face, whereupon she threw up her hands, sank into a chair, and went off into a deep vinous sleep.

___ 5. …at intervals she appeared suddenly at his side like an angry diamond, and hissed: "You promised!" into his ear.

___ 6. A wafer of a moon was shining over Gatsby's house, making the night fine as before, and surviving the laughter and the sound of his still glowing garden.

The Great Gatsby Chapter 3 Figurative Language Page 2

____ 7. Suddenly one of the gypsies, in trembling opal, seizes a cocktail out of the air, dumps it down for courage and, moving her hands like Frisco, dances out alone on the canvas platform.

____ 8. ...but the girls had moved casually on and her remark was addressed to the premature moon, produced like the supper, no doubt, out of a caterer's basket.

____ 9. In the early morning the sun threw my shadow westward as I hurried down the white chasms of lower New York to the Probity Trust.

____ 10. ...while his station wagon scampered like a brisk yellow bug to meet all trains.

The Great Gatsby Chapter 3: Elements of Fiction & Literary Devices

1. The word yellow is used several times in the chapter. What is it primarily associated with?

2. How does Fitzgerald use hyperbole in describing Gatsby's party?

3. Car accidents are mentioned multiple times in this chapter. What is said about them?

4. Consider Nick and Jordan's conversation about car accidents. What might it foreshadow?

5. How does Fitzgerald create suspense around Gatsby's identity and personal history?

6. Compare Owl Eyes' dialogue in the library to his later dialogue at the scene of the car accident. Are they similar? Different? What does his diction suggest about him?

7. How does Gatsby's meeting with Jordan create suspense?

8. What is the "amputated wheel" a symbol of?

The Great Gatsby Chapter 3: Meaning & Inferences 1

Read the passages and answer the related questions.

1. I had been actually invited. A chauffeur in a uniform of robin's-egg blue crossed my lawn early that Saturday morning with a surprisingly formal note from his employer: the honor would be entirely Gatsby's, it said, if I would attend his "little party" that night. He had seen me several times, and had intended to call on me long before, but a peculiar combination of circumstances had prevented it — signed Jay Gatsby, in a majestic hand.

What in the passage conflicts with the idea of a "little party"?

2. As soon as I arrived I made an attempt to find my host, but the two or three people of whom I asked his whereabouts stared at me in such an amazed way, and denied so vehemently any knowledge of his movements, that I slunk off in the direction of the cocktail table — the only place in the garden where a single man could linger without looking purposeless and alone.

What do these reactions suggest that these people feel about Gatsby?

3. Instead of rambling, this party had preserved a dignified homogeneity, and assumed to itself the function of representing the staid nobility of the country-side — East Egg condescending to West Egg, and carefully on guard against its spectroscopic gayety.

What does this suggest about the party-goers' motives for attending the party?

The Great Gatsby Chapter 3 Meaning & Inferences 1 Page 2

4. Something in her tone reminded me of the other girl's "I think he killed a man," and had the effect of stimulating my curiosity. I would have accepted without question the information that Gatsby sprang from the swamps of Louisiana or from the lower East Side of New York. That was comprehensible. But young men didn't — at least in my provincial inexperience I believed they didn't — drift coolly out of nowhere and buy a palace on Long Island Sound.

What isn't "comprehensible" to Nick?

5. Jordan Baker instinctively avoided clever, shrewd men, and now I saw that this was because she felt safer on a plane where any divergence from a code would be thought impossible. She was incurably dishonest. She wasn't able to endure being at a disadvantage and, given this unwillingness, I suppose she had begun dealing in subterfuges when she was very young in order to keep that cool, insolent smile turned to the world and yet satisfy the demands of her hard, jaunty body.

What does this passage reveal about Jordan?

The Great Gatsby Chapter 3: Meaning & Inferences 2

Read the passage and answer the related questions.

"You're a rotten driver," I protested. "Either you ought to be more careful, or you oughtn't to drive at all."

"I am careful."

"No, you're not."

"Well, other people are," she said lightly.

"What's that got to do with it?"

"They'll keep out of my way," she insisted. "It takes two to make an accident."

"Suppose you met somebody just as careless as yourself."

"I hope I never will," she answered. "I hate careless people. That's why I like you."

1. How is Jordan being dishonest in this passage?

2. Is Nick being judgmental in this passage?

3. What causes an accident, according to Jordan? To Nick?

4. What does Jordan rely on to avoid accidents?

5. How is the whole passage a commentary on their relationship? Who is more of a hypocrite, Jordan or Nick?

The Great Gatsby Chapter 3: Who Is Gatsby?

In Chapter 3, after many allusions, the titular character, Jay Gatsby, is finally introduced to the reader. Yet, even after Gatsby is introduced, much about him remains vague.

For this assignment, you will identify passages about Gatsby as a way to form a clearer portrait of who he is and what rumors about him might be true.

To formulate an answer to the question "Who is Gatsby?":

1. Identify passages and quotes about Gatsby.

2. Examine the context of your quotes.

3. Consider the deeper meaning of the quotes:

    a. What is the tone of the speaker—friendly, adversarial, angry, competitive?
    b. Is the claim too exaggerated?
    c. Is there information inferred that is not wholly manifest?

4. Look for patterns in your evidence. Do multiple claims about Gatsby recur?

5. Decide what you believe is true about Gatsby.

The Great Gatsby Chapter 3: Who Is Gatsby?

Complete the chart to analyze information to develop ideas to write your essay.

Quote about or from Gatsby	Tone of the speaker?	Is the claim too exaggerated?	Is there information inferred that is not wholly manifest?

The Great Gatsby Chapter 3: Creative Analytical Writing Assignments

1. Choose your favorite rumor about Gatsby and flesh it out into a whole absurd paragraph.

2. Write a scene with dialogue in which Jordan tells Nick precisely what she thinks of her date.

3. Write Owl Eyes' biography in a paragraph.

4. Write the script of the girls-in-yellows' "baby act." Make sure the content reflects the mores and attitudes of the partygoers.

5. Gatsby says that he is not a good host. Is that true?

6. Write a scene with dialogue of Gatsby talking to "Chicago" "on the wire."

7. Write a meta narrative of what Gatsby is thinking about during the moments as Tostoff's *Jazz History of the World* plays.

8. Write dialogue of Jordan's meeting with Gatsby.

9. Set aside Nick's claim to resist judging people. Write a paragraph from his perspective that honestly reflects how he feels about the people involved in the car accident.

10. Write a love letter from Jordan to Nick, enumerating reasons why she likes him.

The Great Gatsby Chapter 3: Quick-Write Writing Assignments

1. How are Jordan's date and Nick alike and/or different?

2. Describe the attitude of Gatsby's guests towards their host.

3. Compare Gatsby's behavior at his party to his guests' behavior. What does this reveal about Gatsby?

4. The story is set during Prohibition, yet alcohol is served at the party. What role does alcohol play in the chapter?

5. What is the significance of Owl Eyes? Does he have anything in common with T.J. Eckleburg?

6. What are some examples of carelessness in this chapter?

7. Gatsby is introduced through a series of rumors. What effect does this create in the narrative?

8. Why is the automobile wreck significant? What does it reveal about the people who attend Gatsby's parties?

9. Who is honest? Dishonest?

10. Nick describes his personal life/social life and relationship history. What does it reveal about him?

MATERIALS: CHAPTERS 4-5
THE GREAT GATSBY

Reading Activity 1: True or False

Reading Activity 2: Analyzing Passages

Reading Activity 3: Foil Character Study

Reading Activity 4: Action, Character, Decision

Reading Activity 5: Figurative Language

Reading Activity 6: Elements of Fiction & Literary Devices

Reading Activity 7: Meaning and Inferences

Writing Activity 1: How Is Social Class Depicted?

Suggested Writing Assignments

Quick-Write Assignments

NOTES
THE GREAT GATSBY

The Great Gatsby Chapters 4-5: True or False?

Write *True* or *False* in the blank next to each statement. Below the statement, explain why you chose true or false, referencing the text to support your choices.

_____ 1. Gatsby is descended from a prominent Midwestern family.

```
```

_____ 2. Nick is offended by Gatsby's offer of employment.

```
```

_____ 3. Meyer Wolfsheim fixed the World's Series.

```
```

_____ 4. Jordan did not recognize Jay Gatsby when she met him in Long Island.

```
```

The Great Gatsby Chapters 4-5 True or False? Page 2

_____ 5. Daisy got drunk because she believed Gatsby was killed in the war.

_____ 6. Gatsby felt confident about reuniting with Daisy.

The Great Gatsby Chapters 4-5 True or False? Evaluation

List Your Group's Members: Your Group's Question # _____

_____   _____   _____

_____   _____   _____

        1 = No, Not At All 2 = A Little 3 = Some 4 = Yes 5 = Yes, Very Well

Evaluation of Question # ___
Does the explanation support the answer of true or false?	1 2 3 4 5
Is there good textual evidence to support the answer?	1 2 3 4 5
Is the answer clearly stated?	1 2 3 4 5

Total Score _____ of a possible 15 points

Evaluation of Question # ___
Does the explanation support the answer of true or false?	1 2 3 4 5
Is there good textual evidence to support the answer?	1 2 3 4 5
Is the answer clearly stated?	1 2 3 4 5

Total Score _____ of a possible 15 points

Evaluation of Question # ___
Does the explanation support the answer of true or false?	1 2 3 4 5
Is there good textual evidence to support the answer?	1 2 3 4 5
Is the answer clearly stated?	1 2 3 4 5

Total Score _____ of a possible 15 points

Evaluation of Question # ___
Does the explanation support the answer of true or false?	1 2 3 4 5
Is there good textual evidence to support the answer?	1 2 3 4 5
Is the answer clearly stated?	1 2 3 4 5

Total Score _____ of a possible 15 points

Evaluation of Question # ___
Does the explanation support the answer of true or false?	1 2 3 4 5
Is there good textual evidence to support the answer?	1 2 3 4 5
Is the answer clearly stated?	1 2 3 4 5

Total Score _____ of a possible 15 points

The Great Gatsby Chapters 4-5 Analyzing Passages

Answer the questions following the quotations completely.

1. "He was balancing himself on the dashboard of his car with that resourcefulness of movement that is so peculiarly American — that comes, I suppose, with the absence of lifting work or rigid sitting in youth and, even more, with the formless grace of our nervous, sporadic games. This quality was continually breaking through his punctilious manner in the shape of restlessness. He was never quite still; there was always a tapping foot somewhere or the impatient opening and closing of a hand."

    Why is it significant that Gatsby always appears to be in motion?

2. "He looked at me sideways — and I knew why Jordan Baker had believed he was lying. He hurried the phrase "educated at Oxford," or swallowed it, or choked on it, as though it had bothered him before. And with this doubt, his whole statement fell to pieces, and I wondered if there wasn't something a little sinister about him, after all.

    'What part of the Middle West?' I inquired casually.

    'San Francisco.'"

    What is significant about Gatsby's answer?

3. "'Where've you been?' he demanded eagerly. 'Daisy's furious because you haven't called up.'
    'This is Mr. Gatsby, Mr. Buchanan.'
    They shook hands briefly, and a strained, unfamiliar look of embarrassment came over Gatsby's face.
    'How've you been, anyhow?' demanded Tom of me. 'How'd you happen to come up this far to eat?'
    'I've been having lunch with Mr. Gatsby.'
    I turned toward Mr. Gatsby, but he was no longer there."

    Why does Gatsby become embarrassed?

The Great Gatsby Chapters 4-5 Analyzing Passages Page 2

4. "I saw them in Santa Barbara when they came back, and I thought I'd never seen a girl so mad about her husband. If he left the room for a minute she'd look around uneasily, and say: 'Where's Tom gone?' and wear the most abstracted expression until she saw him coming in the door. She used to sit on the sand with his head in her lap by the hour, rubbing her fingers over his eyes and looking at him with unfathomable delight. It was touching to see them together — it made you laugh in a hushed, fascinated way. That was in August. A week after I left Santa Barbara Tom ran into a wagon on the Ventura road one night, and ripped a front wheel off his car. The girl who was with him got into the papers, too, because her arm was broken — she was one of the chambermaids in the Santa Barbara Hotel."

What is Jordan missing about Daisy's behavior? Why is the repetition of Santa Barbara significant?

5. "'Yes.' His eyes went over it, every arched door and square tower. 'It took me just three years to earn the money that bought it.'

'I thought you inherited your money.'

'I did, old sport,' he said automatically, 'but I lost most of it in the big panic — the panic of the war.'

I think he hardly knew what he was saying, for when I asked him what business he was in he answered, 'That's my affair,' before he realized that it wasn't the appropriate reply.

'Oh, I've been in several things,' he corrected himself. 'I was in the drug business and then I was in the oil business. But I'm not in either one now.' He looked at me with more attention. 'Do you mean you've been thinking over what I proposed the other night?'"

What does Gatsby misunderstand?

The Great Gatsby Chapters 4-5 Analyzing Passages Page 3

6. "He took out a pile of shirts and began throwing them, one by one, before us, shirts of sheer linen and thick silk and fine flannel, which lost their folds as they fell and covered the table in many-colored disarray. While we admired he brought more and the soft rich heap mounted higher — shirts with stripes and scrolls and plaids in coral and apple-green and lavender and faint orange, and monograms of Indian blue. Suddenly, with a strained sound, Daisy bent her head into the shirts and began to cry stormily.

   'They're such beautiful shirts,' she sobbed, her voice muffled in the thick folds. 'It makes me sad because I've never seen such — such beautiful shirts before.'"

   Why does Daisy cry?

7. "He hadn't once ceased looking at Daisy, and I think he revalued everything in his house according to the measure of response it drew from her well-loved eyes. Sometimes, too, he stared around at his possessions in a dazed way, as though in her actual and astounding presence none of it was any longer real. Once he nearly toppled down a flight of stairs.
   His bedroom was the simplest room of all — except where the dresser was garnished with a toilet set of pure dull gold. Daisy took the brush with delight, and smoothed her hair, whereupon Gatsby sat down and shaded his eyes and began to laugh."

   Why the emphasis on eyes?

8. "As I went over to say good-by I saw that the expression of bewilderment had come back into Gatsby's face, as though a faint doubt had occurred to him as to the quality of his present happiness. Almost five years! There must have been moments even that afternoon when Daisy tumbled short of his dreams — not through her own fault, but because of the colossal vitality of his illusion. It had gone beyond her, beyond everything. He had thrown himself into it with a creative passion, adding to it all the time, decking it out with every bright feather that drifted his way. No amount of fire or freshness can challenge what a man will store up in his ghostly heart."

   What has Gatsby "stored up?"

The Great Gatsby Chapters 4-5 Reading Activity 3: Foil Character Study

Complete the chart below with quotes from the text that describe Meyer Wolfsheim's interactions with Gatsby and Nick. Consider what these interactions reveal about Wolfsheim as well as about Gatsby and Nick.

Incident	Quotes/Phrases	What does this show about Gatsby?	What does this show about Nick?
Gatsby introducing Wolfsheim to Nick			
On opinions about the old Metropole			
On Gatsby going to Oxford			
On fixing the World's Series			

The Great Gatsby Chapters 4-5: Action, Character, Decision

Write **A** (for Action) **C** (for Character) or **D** (for Decision) in the blank next to each to identify whether the passage/statement advances the action, tells us more about a character, or provokes a decision. On the lines under each question, provide a short explanation of your choice.

____ 1. The officer looked at Daisy while she was speaking, in a way that every young girl wants to be looked at sometime, and because it seemed romantic to me I have remembered the incident ever since.

____ 2. Well, about six weeks ago, she heard the name Gatsby for the first time in years. It was when I asked you — do you remember? — if you knew Gatsby in West Egg. After you had gone home she came into my room and woke me up, and said: "What Gatsby?" and when I described him — I was half asleep — she said in the strangest voice that it must be the man she used to know. It wasn't until then that I connected this Gatsby with the officer in her white car.

____ 3. Gatsby, pale as death, with his hands plunged like weights in his coat pockets, was standing in a puddle of water glaring tragically into my eyes.

____ 4. They were sitting at either end of the couch, looking at each other as if some question had been asked, or was in the air, and every vestige of embarrassment was gone. Daisy's face was smeared with tears, and when I came in she jumped up and began wiping at it with her handkerchief before a mirror. But there was a change in Gatsby that was simply confounding. He literally glowed; without a word or a gesture of exultation a new well-being radiated from him and filled the little room..

____ 5. "Look at that," she whispered, and then after a moment: "I'd like to just get one of those pink clouds and put you in it and push you around."

____ 6. I think that voice held him most, with its fluctuating, feverish warmth, because it couldn't be over-dreamed — that voice was a deathless song..

The Great Gatsby Chapters 4-5: Figurative Language

On the short line provided, write S for simile, M for metaphor, or P for personification. On the lines under each question, explain how the use of figurative language creates meaning.

___ 1. It was a rich cream color, bright with nickel, swollen here and there in its monstrous length with triumphant hat-boxes and supper-boxes and tool-boxes, and terraced with a labyrinth of wind-shields that mirrored a dozen suns.

___ 2. With fenders spread like wings we scattered light through half Long Island City…

___ 3. It never occurred to me that one man could start to play with the faith of fifty million people — with the single-mindedness of a burglar blowing a safe.

___ 4. I had on a new plaid skirt also that blew a little in the wind, and whenever this happened the red, white, and blue banners in front of all the houses stretched out stiff and said tut-tut-tut-tut, in a disapproving way.

___ 5. I came into her room half an hour before the bridal dinner, and found her lying on her bed as lovely as the June night in her flowered dress — and as drunk as a monkey.

___ 6. She took it into the tub with her and squeezed it up into a wet ball, and only let me leave it in the soap-dish when she saw that it was coming to pieces like snow.

The Great Gatsby Chapters 4-5 Figurative Language Page 2

____ 7. At first I thought it was another party, a wild rout that had resolved itself into "hide-and-go-seek" or "sardines-in-the-box" with all the house thrown open to the game.

____ 8. The exhilarating ripple of her voice was a wild tonic in the rain.

____ 9. A damp streak of hair lay like a dash of blue paint across her cheek, and her hand was wet with glistening drops as I took it to help her from the car.

____ 10. As my taxi groaned away I saw Gatsby walking toward me across his lawn.

The Great Gatsby Chapters 4-5: Elements of Fiction & Literary Devices

1. According to Jordan, what happened in October 1917?

2. The flashback to 1917 occurs somewhat abruptly in the middle of Chapter 4, between Nick's lunch with Gatsby and a romantic encounter with Jordan. Is there significance to this juxtaposition?

3. The flashback is recounted from Nick's recollection of hearing the story from Jordan. Why is this choice of perspective significant?

4. Nick's thought, "There are only the pursued, the pursuing, the busy, and the tired." How does this relate to the flashback and Gatsby's scheme, which Jordan is revealing to Nick?

5. Consider the temporal aspects of the plot. What is the primary conflict in Chapters 4 and 5?

6. How does Fitzgerald use the concept of waiting to build suspense in Chapters 4 and 5?

7. In these chapters, characters are not given all the information available in a linear way. Which characters is information withheld from? Why?

The Great Gatsby Chapters 4-5: Meaning & Inferences 1

Read the passages and answer the related questions.

1. From East Egg, then, came the Chester Beckers and the Leeches, and a man named Bunsen, whom I knew at Yale, and Doctor Webster Civet, who was drowned last summer up in Maine. And the Hornbeams and the Willie Voltaires, and a whole clan named Blackbuck, who always gathered in a corner and flipped up their noses like goats at whosoever came near. And the Ismays and the Chrysties (or rather Hubert Auerbach and Mr. Chrystie's wife), and Edgar Beaver, whose hair, they say, turned cotton-white one winter afternoon for no good reason at all.

Clarence Endive was from East Egg, as I remember. He came only once, in white knicker-bockers, and had a fight with a bum named Etty in the garden. From farther out on the Island came the Cheadles and the O. R. P. Schraeders, and the Stonewall Jackson Abrams of Georgia, and the Fishguards and the Ripley Snells. Snell was there three days before he went to the penitentiary, so drunk out on the gravel drive that Mrs. Ulysses Swett's automobile ran over his right hand. The Dancies came, too, and S. B. Whitebait, who was well over sixty, and Maurice A. Flink, and the Hammerheads, and Beluga the tobacco importer, and Beluga's girls.

What is the significance of the list of names?

2. "It was a photograph of half a dozen young men in blazers loafing in an archway through which were visible a host of spires. There was Gatsby, looking a little, not much, younger — with a cricket bat in his hand.

Then it was all true. I saw the skins of tigers flaming in his palace on the Grand Canal; I saw him opening a chest of rubies to ease, with their crimson-lighted depths, the gnawings of his broken heart."

Why does Nick change his mind about Gatsby?

The Great Gatsby Chapters 4-5 Meaning & Inferences 1 Page 2

3. "We passed a barrier of dark trees, and then the facade of Fifty-ninth Street, a block of delicate pale light, beamed down into the park. Unlike Gatsby and Tom Buchanan, I had no girl whose disembodied face floated along the dark cornices and blinding signs, and so I drew up the girl beside me, tightening my arms. Her wan, scornful mouth smiled, and so I drew her up again closer, this time to my face."

How does Nick feel about Jordan?

4. "...They were sitting at either end of the couch looking at each other as if some question had been asked or was in the air, and every vestige of embarrassment was gone. Daisy's face was smeared with tears and when I came in she jumped up and began wiping at it with her handkerchief before a mirror. But there was a change in Gatsby that was simply confounding. He literally glowed; without a word or a gesture of exultation a new well-being radiated from him and filled the little room."

What "question" has likely been asked?

5. "If it wasn't for the mist we could see your home across the bay... You always have a green light that burns all night at the end of your dock."

What is the significance of the proximity and of the mist obscuring the view?

The Great Gatsby Chapters 4-5: Meaning & Inferences 2

Read the passage and answer the related questions.

Gatsby, his hands still in his pockets, was reclining against the mantelpiece in a strained counterfeit of perfect ease, even of boredom. His head leaned back so far that it rested against the face of a defunct mantelpiece clock, and from this position his distraught eyes stared down at Daisy, who was sitting, frightened but graceful, on the edge of a stiff chair.

"We've met before," muttered Gatsby. His eyes glanced momentarily at me, and his lips parted with an abortive attempt at a laugh. Luckily the clock took this moment to tilt dangerously at the pressure of his head, whereupon he turned and caught it with trembling fingers, and set it back in place. Then he sat down, rigidly, his elbow on the arm of the sofa and his chin in his hand.

"I'm sorry about the clock," he said.

My own face had now assumed a deep tropical burn. I couldn't muster up a single commonplace out of the thousand in my head.

"It's an old clock," I told them idiotically.

I think we all believed for a moment that it had smashed in pieces on the floor.

"We haven't met for many years," said Daisy, her voice as matter-of-fact as it could ever be.

"Five years next November."

1. Why is the word "counterfeit" significant?

2. Why is the word "defunct" significant?

3. Why do they believe that the clock broke?

4. What is this scene actually about?

5. Compare Gatsby and Daisy's behavior in the passage.

The Great Gatsby Chapters 4-5:
How Is Social Class Depicted in the Novel?

In Chapters 4-5, many parallels are drawn between Gatsby and a British aristocrat. Fitzgerald is making a commentary on the role of money in society, putting both Nick and the reader in the position of observer of Gatsby's ostentatious show of wealth.

For this assignment, you will identify passages about Gatsby and his wealth, as well as Nick's reflections on his observations, as a way to understand what Fitzgerald is suggesting about money and the upper tier of society who enjoys access to very large sums of money.

To determine an idea about how social class is depicted in the novel:

1. Identify passages and quotes about Gatsby's wealth, especially any references to British aristocracy.

2. Examine the context of your quotes.

3. Consider the deeper meaning of the quotes:

    a. What is the tone—is it positive or negative?
    b. Is the quote advocating for the lifestyle Gatsby lives or cautioning against it?
    c. How do others view Gatsby's wealth?

4. Look for patterns in your evidence. Do multiple opinions about Gatsby's wealth recur?

5. Decide what statement you believe the text is making about social class.

The Great Gatsby Chapters 4-5: How Is Social Class Depicted?

Complete the chart to analyze information to develop ideas to write your essay.

Quote about Gatsby's wealth	Tone: positive or negative?	Does the idea advocate for or caution against Gatsby's lifestyle and class ambition?	How do others view Gatsby's wealth in this passage?

The Great Gatsby Chapters 4-5: Creative Analytical Writing Assignments

1. Write the backstory of Meyer Wolfsheim.
2. Choose one of the stories that Gatsby shares about his past (rubies, Oxford, etc.) and write it out.
3. Write Klipspringer's biography in a paragraph.
4. Describe how Gatsby's car suits him; describe how Daisy's roadster suits her.
5. Write the obituary of the person in the funeral procession.
6. Write a diary entry from Jordan's perspective about why she looked up to Daisy.
7. Write a stream-of-consciousness paragraph of what Daisy thinks when she first sees Gatsby.
8. Imagine Gatsby created a room in the house for Daisy. Describe its contents.
9. Write a poem about the mist and the green light.
10. Write a thank you note from Gatsby to Jordan, thanking her for making the connection to Daisy that he has sought for so long.

The Great Gatsby Chapters 4-5: Quick-Write Writing Assignments

1. What additional details about the place are added as Gatsby and Nick drive through the valley of ashes?

2. In what ways was Daisy disobedient as a girl?

3. What does Jordan think about coincidences?

4. What about Jordan does Nick find attractive?

5. How is Gatsby an actor? Does the "real Gatsby" ever emerge?

6. How does the green light symbolize the American Dream?

7. Is Nick a hypocrite for essentially helping Daisy start an affair, when he did not relish his time with Tom and Myrtle?

8. Can Daisy live up to Gatsby's expectations?

9. What role does love play in a marriage? In an affair?

10. Why is Gatsby reluctant to allow Nick to leave?

MATERIALS: CHAPTERS 6-7
THE GREAT GATSBY

Reading Activity 1: True or False

Reading Activity 2: Analyzing Passages

Reading Activity 3: Static and Dynamic Characters

Reading Activity 4: Action, Character, Decision

Reading Activity 5: Figurative Language

Reading Activity 6: Elements of Fiction & Literary Devices

Reading Activity 7: Meaning and Inferences

Writing Activity 1: Moral Failure In The Great Gatsby

Suggested Writing Assignments

Quick-Write Assignments

NOTES
THE GREAT GATSBY

The Great Gatsby Chapters 6-7: True or False?

Write *True* or *False* in the blank next to each statement. Below the statement, explain why you chose true or false, referencing the text to support your choices.

_____ 1. Gatsby hires organized crime acquaintances to act as domestic servant because of their discretion.

_____ 2. The cause of Wilson's illness is learning that his wife was having an extramarital affair.

_____ 3. Gatsby's wealth was mainly inherited from Dan Cody.

_____ 4. Tom purchased a big, new yellow car.

The Great Gatsby Chapters 6-7 True or False? Page 2

_____ 5. Daisy claims that she never loved Tom at all.

_____ 6. Tom hits Daisy and breaks her nose when he learns that she drove the death car.

The Great Gatsby Chapters 6-7 True or False? Evaluation

List Your Group's Members: Your Group's Question # _____

_____   _____   _____

_____   _____   _____

    1 = No, Not At All **2** = A Little **3** = Some **4** = Yes **5** = Yes, Very Well

Evaluation of Question # ___
Does the explanation support the answer of true or false?	1 2 3 4 5
Is there good textual evidence to support the answer?	1 2 3 4 5
Is the answer clearly stated?	1 2 3 4 5

                    Total Score _____ of a possible 15 points

Evaluation of Question # ___
Does the explanation support the answer of true or false?	1 2 3 4 5
Is there good textual evidence to support the answer?	1 2 3 4 5
Is the answer clearly stated?	1 2 3 4 5

                    Total Score _____ of a possible 15 points

Evaluation of Question # ___
Does the explanation support the answer of true or false?	1 2 3 4 5
Is there good textual evidence to support the answer?	1 2 3 4 5
Is the answer clearly stated?	1 2 3 4 5

                    Total Score _____ of a possible 15 points

Evaluation of Question # ___
Does the explanation support the answer of true or false?	1 2 3 4 5
Is there good textual evidence to support the answer?	1 2 3 4 5
Is the answer clearly stated?	1 2 3 4 5

                    Total Score _____ of a possible 15 points

Evaluation of Question # ___
Does the explanation support the answer of true or false?	1 2 3 4 5
Is there good textual evidence to support the answer?	1 2 3 4 5
Is the answer clearly stated?	1 2 3 4 5

                    Total Score _____ of a possible 15 points

The Great Gatsby Chapters 6-7 Analyzing Passages

Answer the questions following the quotations completely.

1. "I suppose he'd had the name ready for a long time, even then. His parents were shiftless and unsuccessful farm people — his imagination had never really accepted them as his parents at all. The truth was that Jay Gatsby of West Egg, Long Island, sprang from his Platonic conception of himself. He was a son of God — a phrase which, if it means anything, means just that — and he must be about His Father's business, the service of a vast, vulgar, and meretricious beauty. So he invented just the sort of Jay Gatsby that a seventeen-year-old boy would be likely to invent, and to this conception he was faithful to the end."

    The word meretricious means relating to prostitution. What does this usage suggest about Gatsby?

2. "'She has a big dinner party and he won't know a soul there.' He frowned. 'I wonder where in the devil he met Daisy. By God, I may be old-fashioned in my ideas, but women run around too much these days to suit me. They meet all kinds of crazy fish.'"

    Why is this ironic?

3. "It was like that. Almost the last thing I remember was standing with Daisy and watching the moving-picture director and his Star. They were still under the white plum tree and their faces were touching except for a pale, thin ray of moonlight between. It occurred to me that he had been very slowly bending toward her all evening to attain this proximity, and even while I watched I saw him stoop one ultimate degree and kiss at her cheek."

    Why is this significant?

The Great Gatsby Chapters 6-7 Analyzing Passages Page 2

4. "Her glance left me and sought the lighted top of the steps, where *Three O'clock in the Morning*, a neat, sad little waltz of that year, was drifting out the open door. After all, in the very casualness of Gatsby's party there were romantic possibilities totally absent from her world. What was it up there in the song that seemed to be calling her back inside? What would happen now in the dim, incalculable hours? Perhaps some unbelievable guest would arrive, a person infinitely rare and to be marveled at, some authentically radiant young girl who with one fresh glance at Gatsby, one moment of magical encounter, would blot out those five years of unwavering devotion."

What does this suggest about Daisy's state of mind?

5. "His heart beat faster and faster as Daisy's white face came up to his own. He knew that when he kissed this girl, and forever wed his unutterable visions to her perishable breath, his mind would never romp again like the mind of God. So he waited, listening for a moment longer to the tuning-fork that had been struck upon a star. Then he kissed her. At his lips' touch she blossomed for him like a flower and the incarnation was complete."

What is the "incarnation" here? How does Gatsby change?

6. "'She's got an indiscreet voice,' I remarked. 'It's full of ——' I hesitated.'
'Her voice is full of money,' he said suddenly.
That was it. I'd never understood before. It was full of money — that was the inexhaustible charm that rose and fell in it, the jingle of it, the cymbals' song of it. . . . high in a white palace the king's daughter, the golden girl. . ."

What does this suggest about Daisy? About the way Gatsby views her?

The Great Gatsby Chapters 6-7 Analyzing Passages Page 3

7. "The relentless beating heat was beginning to confuse me and I had a bad moment there before I realized that so far his suspicions hadn't alighted on Tom. He had discovered that Myrtle had some sort of life apart from him in another world, and the shock had made him physically sick. I stared at him and then at Tom, who had made a parallel discovery less than an hour before — and it occurred to me that there was no difference between men, in intelligence or race, so profound as the difference between the sick and the well. Wilson was so sick that he looked guilty, unforgivably guilty — as if he had just got some poor girl with child."

   What is the relationship between "sick" and "guilty" here?

8. "Michaelis and this man reached her first, but when they had torn open her shirtwaist, still damp with perspiration, they saw that her left breast was swinging loose like a flap, and there was no need to listen for the heart beneath. The mouth was wide open and ripped at the corners, as though she had choked a little in giving up the tremendous vitality she had stored for so long."

   What does the contrast between her violent death and her life (as Nick imagines it) suggest about Myrtle?

The Great Gatsby Chapters 6-7
Reading Activity 3: Static and Dynamic Characters

A character can be either dynamic or static. A dynamic character grows or progresses in some way as plot in a story moves forward. A static character does not undergo a change and stays fundamentally the same.

From the list of characters below, put the names of two dynamic characters in the relevant boxes and names of two static characters in the relevant boxes. Complete the chart, using actual quotes when asked and noting page numbers. Use your book to locate relevant passages. Note: whether or not some characters are dynamic or static can be debatable; be sure to use compelling textual evidence to support your claims.

Jordan | Nick | Gatsby | Daisy | Tom | Myrtle | Wilson

Dynamic Character	Quote – Observation 1 (Find a quote that shows how a character was before changing. Write the quote below.)	Quote – Observation 2 (Find a quote that shows how a character has undergone change. Write the quote below.)	Describe the Character's Change

Name of Static Character	Quote – Observation 1 (Find a quote that describes a quality or attitude of a static character. Write the quote below.)	Quote – Observation 2 (Find a quote later in the novel that shows that the character has the same quality or attitude. Write the quote below.)	Describe the Character's Quality or Attitude

The Great Gatsby Chapters 6-7: Action, Character, Decision

Write **A** (for Action) **C** (for Character) or **D** (for Decision) in the blank next to each to identify whether the passage/statement advances the action, tells us more about a character, or provokes a decision. On the lines under each question, provide a short explanation of your choice.

____ 1. James Gatz — that was really, or at least legally, his name. He had changed it at the age of seventeen and at the specific moment that witnessed the beginning of his career — when he saw Dan Cody's yacht drop anchor over the most insidious flat on Lake Superior.

____ 2. It was indirectly due to Cody that Gatsby drank so little. Sometimes in the course of gay parties women used to rub champagne into his hair; for himself he formed the habit of letting liquor alone.

____ 3. "Who is this Gatsby anyhow?" demanded Tom suddenly. "Some big bootlegger?"

____ 4. "I wanted somebody who wouldn't gossip. Daisy comes over quite often — in the afternoons."

____ 5. "'You two start on home, Daisy,' said Tom. 'In Mr. Gatsby's car.'
She looked at Tom, alarmed now, but he insisted with magnanimous scorn."

____ 6. "The God damned coward!" he whimpered. "He didn't even stop his car."

The Great Gatsby Chapters 6-7: Figurative Language

Answer the questions that correspond to the letters on the lines below. Explain how the figurative language helps create meaning.

"Come outside," he suggested to Gatsby, "I'd like you to have a look at the place."
I went with them out to the veranda. On the green Sound, stagnant in the heat, one small sail crawled slowly [A] toward the fresher sea. Gatsby's eyes followed it momentarily; he raised his hand and pointed across the bay.
"I'm right across from you."
"So you are."
Our eyes lifted over the rose-beds and the hot lawn and the weedy refuse of the dog-days along-shore [B]. Slowly the white wings of the boat [C] moved against the blue cool limit of the sky [D]. Ahead lay the scalloped ocean and the abounding blessed isles.
"There's sport for you," said Tom, nodding. "I'd like to be out there with him for about an hour."

A. The underlined section is what kind of figurative language?

_____

Why is the mention of a sailboat significant?

B. Consider this visual imagery. What progression does it have?

_____

How does the progression contribute to meaning in the passage? Does it seem positive or negative?

C. The underlined section is what kind of figurative language?

_____

What does the image connote?

The Great Gatsby Chapters 6-7: Figurative Language Page 2

D. The underlined section is what kind of figurative language?
_____

How does this particular action relate to larger themes in the novel?

E. How does the repetition of eyes and eye imagery relate to other points in the novel?

The Great Gatsby Chapters 6-7: Elements of Fiction & Literary Devices

1. One of the motifs in the novel is boats. Consider this passage:

It was a random shot, and yet the reporter's instinct was right. Gatsby's notoriety, spread about by the hundreds who had accepted his hospitality and so become authorities on his past, had increased all summer until he fell just short of being news. Contemporary legends such as the "underground pipe-line to Canada" attached themselves to him, and there was one persistent story that he didn't live in a house at all, but in a boat that looked like a house and was moved secretly up and down the Long Island shore. Just why these inventions were a source of satisfaction to James Gatz of North Dakota, isn't easy to say.

What is the connection between Gatsby and boats? Why is this rumor particularly apt?

2. One of the themes in the novel is becoming a self-made man. How does Gatsby accomplish this, and does it work successfully?

3. A motif in the novel is the weather. What is the weather like in Chapter 7? How does it contribute to meaning?

The Great Gatsby Chapters 6-7: Elements of Fiction & Literary Devices Page 2

4. The concept of perception versus reality is a theme in the novel. In what ways does that appear in Chapter 6 and 7?

5. Why is Gatsby's response to Pammy significant? What does Pammy symbolize?

6. A major theme in the novel is how consumerism corrupts. Is Daisy corrupted? Why is it significant that she compares Gatsby to an advertisement?

The Great Gatsby Chapters 6-7: Meaning & Inferences 1

Read the passages and answer the related questions.

1. "He wanted nothing less of Daisy than that she should go to Tom and say: "I never loved you." After she had obliterated four years with that sentence they could decide upon the more practical measures to be taken. One of them was that, after she was free, they were to go back to Louisville and be married from her house—just as if it were five years ago."

What does returning to Louisville suggest about Gatsby's plans?

2. "I suppose he'd had the name ready for a long time, even then. His parents were shiftless and unsuccessful farm people—his imagination had never really accepted them as his parents at all. The truth was that Jay Gatsby of West Egg, Long Island, sprang from his Platonic conception of himself. He was a son of God – a phrase which, if it means anything, means just that – and he must be about His Father's business, the service of a vast, vulgar, and meretricious beauty. So he invented just the sort of Jay Gatsby that a seventeen-year-old boy would be likely to invent, and to this conception he was faithful to the end."

What, according to Nick, is the "truth" about Gatsby?

The Great Gatsby Chapters 6-7: Meaning & Inferences 1 Page 2

3. "He talked a lot about the past, and I gathered that he wanted to recover something, some idea of himself perhaps, that had gone into loving Daisy. His life had been confused and disordered since then, but if he could return to a certain starting place and go over it all slowly, he could find out what that thing was…"

What "thing" is that?

4. "Thirty – the promise of a decade of loneliness, a thinning list of single men to know, a thinning brief-case of enthusiasm, thinning hair. But there was Jordan beside me, who, unlike Daisy, was too wise ever to carry well-forgotten dreams from age to age. As we passed over the dark bridge her wan face fell lazily against my coat's shoulder and the formidable stroke of thirty died away with the reassuring pressure of her hand."

Why is Nick's recognition about his birthday apropos at this moment?

5. "She's not leaving me!" Tom's words suddenly leaned down over Gatsby. "Certainly not for a common swindler who'd have to steal the ring he put on her finger."

"I won't stand this!" cried Daisy. "Oh, please let's get out."

What does this suggest about Tom's view of marriage?

The Great Gatsby Chapters 6-7: Meaning & Inferences 2

Read the passage and answer the related questions.

I hadn't gone twenty yards when I heard my name and Gatsby stepped from between two bushes into the path. I must have felt pretty weird by that time because I could think of nothing except the luminosity of his pink suit under the moon.

    'What are you doing?' I inquired.
    'Just standing here, old sport.'
    Somehow that seemed a despicable occupation. For all I knew he was going to rob the house in a moment; I wouldn't have been surprised to see sinister faces, the faces of "Wolfsheim's people," behind him in the dark shrubbery.
    "Did you see any trouble on the road?" he asked after a minute.
    "Yes."
    He hesitated.
    "Was she killed?"
    "Yes."
    "I thought so; I told Daisy I thought so. It's better that the shock should all come at once. She stood it pretty well."
    He spoke as if Daisy's reaction was the only thing that mattered.

1. What does the "luminosity" of Gatsby's suit connote?

2. What might "weird" suggest?

3. Why is it a "despicable occupation"?

4. How does Nick feel towards Gatsby here?

5. What does "as if" suggest about Nick's view of the night's events?

The Great Gatsby Chapters 6-7:
How Is Moral Failure Significant In The Great Gatsby?

As the omniscient eyes of T.J. Eckleburg loom over the bleak landscape of the Valley of Ashes, moral failure is a major theme in the novel. Though the narrator of the story claims to reserve judgment, the reader can detect that Nick understands that the characters surrounding him all participate in morally questionable acts.

Through close reading of the text, determine what the significance of moral failure in the novel is. Do all characters suffer the repercussions of their actions? Why or why not?

Using textual evidence from chapters 6-7, look for important but perhaps seemingly insignificant details to answer to the question: How is moral failure significant in The Great Gatsby?

To explore the significance of moral failure:

1. Identify passages and quotes which offer details or insights into how characters view their own morally questionable behaviors and if/when they suffer consequences of their behaviors.

2. Examine the context of your quotes.

3. Consider the connotation and denotation of key phrases in your quotes.

    a. Are there judgmental words or phrases?
    b. Does who a character interacts with matter?
    c. How does social class fit into excusing or punishing morally questionably behavior?
    d. Consider the perspective of the narrator. Is it biased?

4. Review passages for patterns to determine what the significance of moral failure is.

The Great Gatsby Chapters 6-7:
What Is The Significance Of Moral Failure In The Great Gatsby?

Use this chart (and additional pages, if needed) to collect, analyze and evaluate information about the trial.

Character	What moral transgressions has this character committed? Include textual evidence and page numbers.	Does the character (or other characters) justify their actions? How? Include textual evidence and page numbers.	Is there any consequence for the character's morally questionable behavior? Include textual evidence and page numbers.
Gatsby			
Nick			
Daisy			
Tom			

The Great Gatsby Chapters 6-7: Creative Analytical Writing Assignments

1. Write a letter from Gatsby at college home to his parents. Incorporate details from the text.

2. Write a eulogy by Gatsby for Dan Cody.

3. Write a scene between Gatsby and Nick in which Gatsby explains why he does not drink alcohol.

4. Write a description of the past that Gatsby wants to repeat.

5. Write a letter from Daisy to Pammy about how to choose a husband.

6. Describe the life out west that Myrtle dreamed about when she was more happily married.

7. Write a newspaper account of Myrtle's accident.

8. Write an account of what happened that caused Tom and Daisy to leave Chicago.

9. During the confrontation between Gatsby and Tom at the hotel, write a paragraph that describes what Jordan is thinking.

10. Write the dialogue between Tom and Daisy as they are in their kitchen during the night of the accident.

The Great Gatsby Chapters 6-7: Quick-Write Writing Assignments

1. Why doesn't Daisy like Gatsby's party?
2. Why did Gatsby drop out of college?
3. Does Gatsby really love Daisy?
4. Who treats Daisy more like a possession, Gatsby or Tom?
5. What is Nick unable to vocalize at the end of Chapter 6?
6. What do Wilson and Tom have in common?
7. How does the green light symbolize the American Dream?
8. Why does Gatsby defend his business against Tom's criticisms?
9. Which is a more important mentor for Gatsby: Dan Cody or Meyer Wolfsheim?
10. When Nick sees Tom and Daisy in their kitchen talking, what does he recognize that this means for Gatsby's dream?

NOTES
THE GREAT GATSBY

MATERIALS: CHAPTERS 8-9
THE GREAT GATSBY

Reading Activity 1: True or False

Reading Activity 2: Analyzing Passages

Reading Activity 3: Direct And Indirect Characterization

Reading Activity 4: Action, Character, Decision

Reading Activity 5: Figurative Language

Reading Activity 6: Elements of Fiction & Literary Devices

Reading Activity 7: Meaning and Inferences

Writing Activity 1: Is Nick A Reliable Narrator?

Suggested Writing Assignments

Quick-Write Assignments

NOTES
THE GREAT GATSBY

The Great Gatsby Chapters 8-9: True or False?

Write *True* or *False* in the blank next to each statement. Below the statement, explain why you chose true or false, referencing the text to support your choices.

_____ 1. Gatsby wanted to be at Oxford.

_____ 2. After the war, Gatsby returned to Louisville.

_____ 3. Nick actually disapproved of Gatsby.

The Great Gatsby Chapters 8-9 True or False? Page 2

_____ 4. Nick says he was just an acquaintance of Gatsby.

_____ 5. Tom believes that Gatsby got what he deserved.

_____ 6. Owl-eyes is an unexpected attendee at Gatsby's burial.

The Great Gatsby Chapters 8-9 True or False? Evaluation

List Your Group's Members:　　　　　　Your Group's Question # _____

_____　　_____　　_____

_____　　_____　　_____

1 = No, Not At All **2** = A Little **3** = Some **4** = Yes **5** = Yes, Very Well

Evaluation of Question # ___
Does the explanation support the answer of true or false?　　1 2 3 4 5
Is there good textual evidence to support the answer?　　　　1 2 3 4 5
Is the answer clearly stated?　　　　　　　　　　　　　　　1 2 3 4 5
　　　　　　　　　　　　　　Total Score _____ of a possible 15 points

Evaluation of Question # ___
Does the explanation support the answer of true or false?　　1 2 3 4 5
Is there good textual evidence to support the answer?　　　　1 2 3 4 5
Is the answer clearly stated?　　　　　　　　　　　　　　　1 2 3 4 5
　　　　　　　　　　　　　　Total Score _____ of a possible 15 points

Evaluation of Question # ___
Does the explanation support the answer of true or false?　　1 2 3 4 5
Is there good textual evidence to support the answer?　　　　1 2 3 4 5
Is the answer clearly stated?　　　　　　　　　　　　　　　1 2 3 4 5
　　　　　　　　　　　　　　Total Score _____ of a possible 15 points

Evaluation of Question # ___
Does the explanation support the answer of true or false?　　1 2 3 4 5
Is there good textual evidence to support the answer?　　　　1 2 3 4 5
Is the answer clearly stated?　　　　　　　　　　　　　　　1 2 3 4 5
　　　　　　　　　　　　　　Total Score _____ of a possible 15 points

Evaluation of Question # ___
Does the explanation support the answer of true or false?　　1 2 3 4 5
Is there good textual evidence to support the answer?　　　　1 2 3 4 5
Is the answer clearly stated?　　　　　　　　　　　　　　　1 2 3 4 5
　　　　　　　　　　　　　　Total Score _____ of a possible 15 points

The Great Gatsby Chapters 8-9 Analyzing Passages

Answer the questions following the quotations completely.

1. "I couldn't sleep all night; a fog-horn was groaning incessantly on the Sound, and I tossed half-sick between grotesque reality and savage, frightening dreams. Toward dawn I heard a taxi go up Gatsby's drive, and immediately I jumped out of bed and began to dress — I felt that I had something to tell him, something to warn him about, and morning would be too late."

    How does this suggest foreshadowing?

2. "It was this night that he told me the strange story of his youth with Dan Cody — told it to me because 'Jay Gatsby' had broken up like glass against Tom's hard malice, and the long secret extravaganza was played out. I think that he would have acknowledged anything now, without reserve, but he wanted to talk about Daisy."

    Why is "acknowledged" significant here?

3. "It excited him, too, that many men had already loved Daisy — it increased her value in his eyes. He felt their presence all about the house, pervading the air with the shades and echoes of still vibrant emotions."

    What does this suggest about how Gatsby views Daisy?

The Great Gatsby Chapters 8-9 Analyzing Passages Page 2

4. "I can't describe to you how surprised I was to find out I loved her, old sport. I even hoped for a while that she'd throw me over, but she didn't, because she was in love with me too. She thought I knew a lot because I knew different things from her. . . . Well, there I was, 'way off my ambitions, getting deeper in love every minute, and all of a sudden I didn't care. What was the use of doing great things if I could have a better time telling her what I was going to do?"

What does this show about how Gatsby relates to time?

5. "I wanted to get somebody for him. I wanted to go into the room where he lay and reassure him: 'I'll get somebody for you, Gatsby. Don't worry. Just trust me and I'll get somebody for you ——'"

Why does Nick want to "get somebody" for Gatsby? What does that mean?

6. "Next morning I sent the butler to New York with a letter to Wolfsheim, which asked for information and urged him to come out on the next train. That request seemed superfluous when I wrote it. I was sure he'd start when he saw the newspapers, just as I was sure there'd be a wire from Daisy before noon — but neither a wire nor Mr. Wolfsheim arrived; no one arrived except more police and photographers and newspaper men. When the butler brought back Wolfsheim's answer I began to have a feeling of defiance, of scornful solidarity between Gatsby and me against them all."

What does Nick feel "defian[t]" about?

The Great Gatsby Chapters 8-9 Analyzing Passages Page 3

7. "After that I felt a certain shame for Gatsby — one gentleman to whom I telephoned implied that he had got what he deserved. However, that was my fault, for he was one of those who used to sneer most bitterly at Gatsby on the courage of Gatsby's liquor, and I should have known better than to call him."

   What specifically does Nick feel shame about?

8. "You said a bad driver was only safe until she met another bad driver? Well, I met another bad driver, didn't I? I mean it was careless of me to make such a wrong guess. I thought you were rather an honest, straightforward person. I thought it was your secret pride."

   What is Jordan intimating about Nick?

The Great Gatsby Chapters 8-9
Reading Activity 3: Direct vs. Indirect Characterization

Characterization, or the development of characters in a work of fiction, can be direct or indirect. Direct characterization is revealing aspects of character directly to the reader via a narrator, the character him or herself or from another character. Indirect characterization requires readers to infer what a character is like through the character's thoughts, action, diction, appearance and interactions with others.

Complete the chart, using actual quotes when asked and noting page numbers.

Character	Direct Characterization Quote	Indirect Characterization Quote	Indirect Characterization Inference
Nick			
Gatsby			
Tom			
Wilson			
Jordan			
Wolfsheim			
Owl-eyes			

The Great Gatsby Chapters 8-9: Action, Character, Decision

Write **A** (for Action) **C** (for Character) or **D** (for Decision) in the blank next to each to identify whether the passage/statement advances the action, tells us more about a character, or provokes a decision. On the lines under each question, provide a short explanation of your choice.

____ 1. "As a matter of fact, he had no such facilities — he had no comfortable family standing behind him, and he was liable at the whim of an impersonal government to be blown anywhere about the world."

____ 2. "He had intended, probably, to take what he could and go — but now he found that he had committed himself to the following of a grail."

____ 3. "And all the time something within her was crying for a decision. She wanted her life shaped now, immediately — and the decision must be made by some force — of love, of money, of unquestionable practicality — that was close at hand."

____ 4. "When the butler brought back Wolfsheim's answer I began to have a feeling of defiance, of scornful solidarity between Gatsby and me against them all."

____ 5. "'I don't think she ever loved him.' Gatsby turned around from a window and looked at me challengingly."

____ 6. "'I can't do it — I can't get mixed up in it,' he said."

The Great Gatsby Chapters 8-9: Figurative Language

Irony is the contrast between what is expected or what appears to be and what actually is. Irony can be verbal (a contrast using language) or situational (a contrast using an unexpected result). Explain how irony helps create meaning in the passages below

1. His gorgeous pink rag of a suit made a bright spot of color against the white steps, and I thought of the night when I first came to his ancestral home, three months before.

___

2. The minister glanced several times at his watch, so I took him aside and asked him to wait for half an hour. But it wasn't any use. Nobody came.

___

3. "If he'd of lived, he'd of been a great man. A man like James J. Hill. He'd of helped build up the country."
"That's true," I said, uncomfortably.

___

4. "I couldn't get to the house," he remarked.
"Neither could anybody else."
"Go on!" He started. "Why, my God! they used to go there by the hundreds." He took off his glasses and wiped them again, outside and in.

___

5. "What I called up about was a pair of shoes I left there. I wonder if it'd be too much trouble to have the butler send them on. You see, they're tennis shoes, and I'm sort of helpless without them. My address is care of B. F. ——"

___

The Great Gatsby Chapters 8-9: Elements of Fiction & Literary Devices

1. One of the motifs in the novel is the weather. At what point in the season does this chapter take place? With what details does Fitzgerald convey that?

2. Chapters 8 and 9 have the most interruptions by Nick that draw attention to his role as narrator. Explain the significance of this shift in perspective: "Now I want to go back a little and tell what happened at the garage after we left there the night before"

3. Consider the motif of seeing and eyes in the novel. Assess this quote:

"Standing behind him, Michaelis saw with a shock that he was looking at the eyes of Doctor T. J. Eckleburg, which had just emerged, pale and enormous, from the dissolving night.
'God sees everything,' repeated Wilson.
'That's an advertisement,' Michaelis assured him."

Does Wilson's understanding of Doctor T. J. Eckleburg align with the general idea of the motif or diverge from it?

4. Compare this scene to the scene where Nick attempts (and succeeds) to gain access to Meyer Wolfsheim. What does the difference between these encounters suggest about the very wealthy?

"I called up Daisy half an hour after we found him, called her instinctively and without hesitation. But she and Tom had gone away early that afternoon, and taken baggage with them.
'Left no address?'
'No.'
'Say when they'd be back?'
'No.'
'Any idea where they are? How I could reach them?'
'I don't know. Can't say.'"

The Great Gatsby Chapters 8-9: Elements of Fiction & Literary Devices Page 2

5. How does Mr, Gatz reflect the American Dream?

6. What is the source of the conflict between Nick and Jordan?

The Great Gatsby Chapters 8-9: Meaning & Inferences 1

Read the passages and answer the related questions.

1. He knew that Daisy was extraordinary, but he didn't realize just how extraordinary a "nice" girl could be. She vanished into her rich house, into her rich, full life, leaving Gatsby — nothing. He felt married to her, that was all.

What is the definition of marriage here?

2. "Wilson's glazed eyes turned out to the ashheaps, where small gray clouds took on fantastic shape and scurried here and there in the faint dawn wind."

What does this suggest about Wilson's state of mind?

3. "'Tom,' I inquired, 'what did you say to Wilson that afternoon?' He stared at me without a word, and I knew I had guessed right about those missing hours. I started to turn away, but he took a step after me and grabbed my arm."

What has Nick "guessed right about"? What is Tom's attitude about that?

The Great Gatsby Chapters 8-9: Meaning & Inferences 1 Page 2

4. "On the last night, with my trunk packed and my car sold to the grocer, I went over and looked at that huge incoherent failure of a house once more. On the white steps an obscene word, scrawled by some boy with a piece of brick, stood out clearly in the moonlight, and I erased it, drawing my shoe raspingly along the stone. Then I wandered down to the beach and sprawled out on the sand."

What is Nick trying to preserve here? Why?

5. "I couldn't forgive him or like him, but I saw that what he had done was, to him, entirely justified. It was all very careless and confused. They were careless people, Tom and Daisy — they smashed up things and creatures and then retreated back into their money or their vast carelessness, or whatever it was that kept them together, and let other people clean up the mess they had made. . . ."

What is the significance of the ellipses here?

The Great Gatsby Chapters 8-9: Meaning & Inferences 2

Read the passage and answer the related questions.

"They're a rotten crowd," I shouted across the lawn. "You're worth the whole damn bunch put together."

I've always been glad I said that. It was the only compliment I ever gave him, because I disapproved of him from beginning to end. First he nodded politely, and then his face broke into that radiant and understanding smile, as if we'd been in ecstatic cahoots on that fact all the time. His gorgeous pink rag of a suit made a bright spot of color against the white steps, and I thought of the night when I first came to his ancestral home, three months before. The lawn and drive had been crowded with the faces of those who guessed at his corruption-and he had stood on those steps, concealing his incorruptible dream, as he waved them good-by.

I thanked him for his hospitality. We were always thanking him for that-I and the others.

"Good-by," I called. "I enjoyed breakfast, Gatsby."

1. How does this passage make Nick a hypocrite?

2. What do the words "crowd" and "bunch" signify?

3. What is the difference between Gatsby's polite nod and "radiant and understanding smile"?

4. How do the words "corruption" and "incorruptible" work together in the passage?

5. What is the overall tone of the passage?

The Great Gatsby Chapters 8-9: Is Nick A Reliable Narrator?

F. Scott Fitzgerald employs a relatively minor, ancillary character to convey the story of the title character through first-person narration. Information about Gatsby and his world is filtered through Nick, who claims to be both honest and non-judgmental. Through close reading of the text, determine whether Nick is a reliable narrator, and how your answer to that question affects the way meaning is perceived in the novel. How does Nick's role as narrator affect a larger understanding of the plot and characters? How does Nick's perspective shift the novel?

Using textual evidence from chapters 8-9, look for key moments in the narration to answer the question: Is Nick a reliable narrator?

To explore this question:

1. Identify passages and quotes which exemplify Nick in his role as narrator, particularly moments when he directly interrupts the text and draws attention to storytelling.

2. Examine the context of your quotes.

3. Consider the connotation and denotation of key phrases in your quotes.

   a. Are there judgmental words or phrases?
   b. What does Nick suggest about his role as narrator?
   c. Do Nick's observations fit with his moral code (honest, non-judgmental)?
   d. Is Nick explaining why or how he is telling Gatsby's story?

4. Review passages for patterns to determine what the significance of Nick's reliability as narrator is.

The Great Gatsby Chapter 8-9: Is Nick A Reliable Narrator?

Use this chart (and additional pages, if needed) to collect, analyze and evaluate information about Nick as narrator.

Observation from the text (quotes)	Paraphrase quote	Is the quote biased or judgmental in any way?	What does the quote suggest about Nick as a narrator?

The Great Gatsby Chapters 8-9: Creative Analytical Writing Assignments

1. Write a newspaper report of the murder/suicide incident on Gatsby's property.

2. Write a eulogy for Gatsby by Nick.

3. Write a paragraph which expresses Daisy's thoughts when she learns that Gatsby has been murdered.

4. Write dialogue from Catherine that explains what she knew about her sister's life—make it true or use discretion.

5. Write a description of the West that urges people who moved East to return home.

6. Describe the trip that Tom and Daisy hastily take.

7. Imagine Gatsby had a will. What objects might he leave to Nick?

8. Write a book review of "Nick's book," with an awareness of the scandalous news of Gatsby and Wilson.

9. Why does Nick feel compelled to write a book about Gatsby? Write an epilogue to "Nick's book" that explains why.

10. Write a poem inspired by the last line of the novel: So we beat on, boats against the current, borne back ceaselessly into the past.

The Great Gatsby Chapters 8-9: Quick-Write Writing Assignments

1. Why is Nick unable to sleep at the beginning of Chapter 8? How does that connect with larger themes in the novel?

2. What does Nick's compliment to Gatsby suggest about Nick's propensity not to judge others?

3. What does Klipspringer represent?

4. How does Wilson view and understand T.J. Eckleburg? How does Michaelis respond?

5. Why does Nick become the spokesperson for Gatsby's estate? Why does he arrange the funeral?

6. What do Gatsby and his father have in common?

7. Is Wilson a mad man?

8. Is Gatsby's funeral similar to his parties? If so, how? If not, why not?

9. Was Nick's relationship with Jordan destined to fail? Why?

10. If Tom believes that Gatsby got what he deserved, by the same logic, did Myrtle or Tom get what they deserved?

MATERIALS: OVERVIEW
THE GREAT GATSBY

Reading Activity 1: True or False

Reading Activity 2: Analyzing Passages

Reading Activity 3: Character Culpability

Reading Activity 4: Action, Character, Decision

Reading Activity 5: Figurative Language

Reading Activity 6: Elements of Fiction & Literary Devices

Reading Activity 7: Meaning and Inferences

Writing Activity 1: Moral Failure In The Great Gatsby

Suggested Writing Assignments

Quick-Write Assignments

NOTES
THE GREAT GATSBY

The Great Gatsby Overview: True or False?

Write *True* or *False* in the blank next to each statement. Below the statement, explain why you chose true or false, referencing the text to support your choices.

_____ 1. Daisy never loved Tom.

```
┌─────────────────────────────────────────────────────────────┐
│                                                             │
│                                                             │
│                                                             │
│                                                             │
└─────────────────────────────────────────────────────────────┘
```

_____ 2. Daisy is directly responsible for Myrtle's death.

```
┌─────────────────────────────────────────────────────────────┐
│                                                             │
│                                                             │
│                                                             │
│                                                             │
└─────────────────────────────────────────────────────────────┘
```

_____ 3. Nick notes that Gatsby's funeral was as well attended as his parties.

```
┌─────────────────────────────────────────────────────────────┐
│                                                             │
│                                                             │
│                                                             │
│                                                             │
└─────────────────────────────────────────────────────────────┘
```

The Great Gatsby Overview True or False? Page 2

_____ 4. Gatsby became interested in self-improvement only after meeting Dan Cody.

_____ 5. Daisy's hope for her daughter is that she grows up to be a fool.

_____ 6. Ultimately, Jordan believes that Nick is neither honest nor straightforward.

The Great Gatsby Overview True or False? Evaluation

List Your Group's Members:　　　　　Your Group's Question # _____

_____　　_____　　_____

_____　　_____　　_____

1 = No, Not At All **2** = A Little **3** = Some **4** = Yes **5** = Yes, Very Well

Evaluation of Question # ___
Does the explanation support the answer of true or false?　　1 2 3 4 5
Is there good textual evidence to support the answer?　　　　1 2 3 4 5
Is the answer clearly stated?　　　　　　　　　　　　　　　1 2 3 4 5
　　　　　　　　　　　Total Score _____ of a possible 15 points

Evaluation of Question # ___
Does the explanation support the answer of true or false?　　1 2 3 4 5
Is there good textual evidence to support the answer?　　　　1 2 3 4 5
Is the answer clearly stated?　　　　　　　　　　　　　　　1 2 3 4 5
　　　　　　　　　　　Total Score _____ of a possible 15 points

Evaluation of Question # ___
Does the explanation support the answer of true or false?　　1 2 3 4 5
Is there good textual evidence to support the answer?　　　　1 2 3 4 5
Is the answer clearly stated?　　　　　　　　　　　　　　　1 2 3 4 5
　　　　　　　　　　　Total Score _____ of a possible 15 points

Evaluation of Question # ___
Does the explanation support the answer of true or false?　　1 2 3 4 5
Is there good textual evidence to support the answer?　　　　1 2 3 4 5
Is the answer clearly stated?　　　　　　　　　　　　　　　1 2 3 4 5
　　　　　　　　　　　Total Score _____ of a possible 15 points

Evaluation of Question # ___
Does the explanation support the answer of true or false?　　1 2 3 4 5
Is there good textual evidence to support the answer?　　　　1 2 3 4 5
Is the answer clearly stated?　　　　　　　　　　　　　　　1 2 3 4 5
　　　　　　　　　　　Total Score _____ of a possible 15 points

The Great Gatsby Overview Analyzing Passages

Answer the questions following the quotations completely.

1. "He had one of those rare smiles with a quality of eternal reassurance in it that you may come across four or five times in life. It faced, or seemed to face, the whole external world for an instant and then concentrated on you with an irresistible prejudice in your favor. It understood you just as far as you wanted to be understood, believed in you as you would like to believe in yourself."

   What does the quality of Gatsby's smile reflect about his own hopes?

2. "That's my Middle West — not the wheat or the prairies or the lost Swede towns, but the thrilling returning trains of my youth, and the street lamps and sleigh bells in the frosty dark and the shadows of holly wreaths thrown by lighted windows on the snow. I am part of that, a little solemn with the feel of those long winters, a little complacent from growing up in the Carraway house in a city where dwellings are still called through decades by a family's name. I see now that this has been a story of the West, after all — Tom and Gatsby, Daisy and Jordan and I, were all Westerners, and perhaps we possessed some deficiency in common which made us subtly unadaptable to Eastern life." What makes their story "a story of the West?"

   What does that mean?

3. "He was content to be alone--he stretched out his arms toward the dark water in a curious way, and as far as I was from him, I could have sworn he was trembling. Involuntarily I glanced seaward--and distinguished nothing except a single green light."

   Is Gatsby alone? Explain your answer.

The Great Gatsby Overview Analyzing Passages Page 2

4. "Almost five years! There must have been moments even that afternoon when Daisy tumbled short of his dreams--not through her own fault, but because of the colossal vitality of his illusion. It had gone beyond her, beyond everything. He had thrown himself into it with a creative passion, adding to it all the time, decking it out with every bright feather that drifted his way."

What does the repetition of "beyond" suggest?

5. "But he didn't despise himself and it didn't turn out as he had imagined. He had intended, probably, to take what he could and go-but now he found that he had committed himself to the following of a grail. He knew that Daisy was extraordinary, but he didn't realize just how extraordinary a "nice" girl could be. She vanished into her rich house, into her rich, full life, leaving Gatsby-nothing. He felt married to her, that was all."

What is significant about the tone of the last line?

6. "'She's got an indiscreet voice,' I remarked. 'It's full of ——' I hesitated.'
'Her voice is full of money,' he said suddenly.
That was it. I'd never understood before. It was full of money — that was the inexhaustible charm that rose and fell in it, the jingle of it, the cymbals' song of it. . . . high in a white palace the king's daughter, the golden girl. . ."

What does this suggest about Daisy? About the way Gatsby views her?

The Great Gatsby Overview Analyzing Passages Page 3

7. "Some time toward midnight Tom Buchanan and Mrs. Wilson stood face to face discussing, in impassioned voices, whether Mrs. Wilson had any right to mention Daisy's name. 'Daisy! Daisy! Daisy!' shouted Mrs. Wilson. 'I'll say it whenever I want to! Daisy! Dai —'

Making a short deft movement, Tom Buchanan broke her nose with his open hand."

What is the significance of using full and formal names?

8. "'I spoke to her,' he muttered, after a long silence. 'I told her she might fool me but she couldn't fool God. I took her to the window.'— with an effort he got up and walked to the rear window and leaned with his face pressed against it ——'and I said 'God knows what you've been doing, everything you've been doing. You may fool me, but you can't fool God!"

Standing behind him, Michaelis saw with a shock that he was looking at the eyes of Doctor T. J. Eckleburg, which had just emerged, pale and enormous, from the dissolving night.

'God sees everything,' repeated Wilson.

'That's an advertisement,' Michaelis assured him. Something made him turn away from the window and look back into the room. But Wilson stood there a long time, his face close to the window pane, nodding into the twilight."

What is significant about T.J. Eckleburg being an advertisement?

The Great Gatsby Overview Reading Activity 3: Character Culpability

Sometimes in literature, the heroes and villains of a story are clear. In this novel, morally ambiguous behavior makes determining the characters' culpability for the downfall of others more complicated.

Consider the ultimate outcomes for Gatsby and Myrtle. Which characters are most culpable for these outcomes?

Rank the main characters on a continuum based on textual evidence of how culpable they are for the tragic outcomes. Jot down reasons to justify your rankings.

Jordan | Nick | Gatsby | Daisy | Tom | Myrtle | Wilson

LEAST CULPABLE

Name	Reason For Ranking In This Place

MOST CULPABLE

The Great Gatsby Overview: Action, Character, Decision

Write **A** (for Action) **C** (for Character) or **D** (for Decision) in the blank next to each to identify whether the passage/statement advances the action, tells us more about a character, or provokes a decision. On the lines under each question, provide a short explanation of your choice.

___ 1. On the other hand, no garage man who had seen him ever came forward, and perhaps he had an easier, surer way of finding out what he wanted to know.

___ 2. "And Daisy ought to have something in her life," murmured Jordan to me.

___ 3. Two shining arrogant eyes had established dominance over his face and gave him the appearance of always leaning aggressively forward. Not even the effeminate swank of his riding clothes could hide the enormous power of that body — he seemed to fill those glistening boots until he strained the top lacing, and you could see a great pack of muscle shifting when his shoulder moved under his thin coat. It was a body capable of enormous leverage — a cruel body.

___ 4. I think it was on the third day that a telegram signed Henry C. Gatz arrived from a town in Minnesota. It said only that the sender was leaving immediately and to postpone the funeral until he came.

___ 5. "Jimmy was bound to get ahead. He always had some resolves like this or something. Do you notice what he's got about improving his mind? He was always great for that. He told me I et like a hog once, and I beat him for it."

___ 6. "Miss Baker?" he inquired. "I beg your pardon, but Mr. Gatsby would like to speak to you alone."

The Great Gatsby Overview: Figurative Language

On the short line provided, write **S** for simile, **M** for metaphor or **I** for idiom. On the lines under each question, explain the meaning and specifically how the figurative language helps create meaning.

___ 1. "She took it into the tub with her and squeezed it up into a wet ball, and only let me leave it in the soap-dish when she saw that it was coming to pieces like snow."

___ 2. "I've got my hands full."

___ 3. "<u>This is a valley of ashes — a fantastic farm</u> where ashes grow like wheat into ridges and hills and grotesque gardens; where ashes take the forms of houses and chimneys and rising smoke and, finally, with a transcendent effort, of men who move dimly and already crumbling through the powdery air."

___ 4. "This is a valley of ashes — a fantastic farm where <u>ashes grow like wheat</u> into ridges and hills and grotesque gardens; where ashes take the forms of houses and chimneys and rising smoke and, finally, with a transcendent effort, of men who move dimly and already crumbling through the powdery air."

___ 5. "The only completely stationary object in the room was an enormous couch on which two young women were buoyed up as though upon an anchored balloon."

The Great Gatsby Overview: Elements of Fiction & Literary Devices

1. Throughout the book, the theme of being "self-made" plays a large role. In what ways does this theme show up throughout Gatsby's actions?

2. Refer to the passage below:

> "She's got an indiscreet voice," I remarked. "It's full of——" I hesitated.
>
> "Her voice is full of money," he said suddenly.
>
> That was it. I'd never understood before. It was full of money—that was the inexhaustible charm that rose and fell in it, the jingle of it, the cymbals' song of it. . . . high in a white palace the king's daughter, the golden girl. . . (120)

This passage depicts a couple of different themes that are portrayed throughout the book. Select one and connect this passage to another moment in the novel.

3. Consumerism and materialism are themes in the novel. How do Gatsby's material possessions reflect his moral values? Refer to at least 2 different individual items owned by Gatsby/Gatz that are mentioned in the novel.

The Great Gatsby Overview: Elements of Fiction & Literary Devices Page 2

4. Refer to the passage below:

> The "death car." as the newspapers called it, didn't stop; it came out of the gathering darkness, wavered tragically for a moment, and then disappeared around the next bend. (137)

Relate the above passage to Gatsby's life.

5. What does the green light symbolize?

6. One of the novel's motifs is sports. Consider the role this motif plays in the novel and its significance.

The Great Gatsby Overview: Meaning & Inferences 1

Read the passages and answer the related questions.

1. Refer to the passage below:

> "Meyer Wolfshiem? No, he's a gambler." Gatsby hesitated, then added coolly: "He's the man who fixed the World's Series back in 1919."
>
> "Fixed the World's Series?" I repeated.
>
> The idea staggered me. I remembered, of course, that the World's Series had been fixed in 1919, but if I had thought of it at all I would have thought of it as a thing that merely HAPPENED, the end of some inevitable chain. It never occurred to me that one man could start to play with the faith of fifty million people—with the single-mindedness of a burglar blowing a safe.
>
> "How did he happen to do that?" I asked after a minute.
>
> "He just saw the opportunity."

What does this passage reveal about Nick's characterization?

2. Refer to the passage below:

> In my younger and more vulnerable years my father gave me some advice that I've been turning over in my mind ever since.
>
> "Whenever you feel like criticizing any one," he told me, "just remember that all the people in this world haven't had the advantages that you've had."

Does Nick follow this advice or not? Why is this significant?

The Great Gatsby Overview: Meaning & Inferences 1 Page 2

3. Refer to the passage below:

> The other car, the one going toward <u>New York</u>, came to rest a hundred yards beyond, and its driver hurried back to where Myrtle <u>Wilson</u>, her life violently extinguished, knelt in the road and mingled her thick dark blood with the <u>dust</u>. (137)

Respond to the quote above, focusing specifically on one of the words underlined above.

4. Refer to the passage below:

> His parents were shiftless and unsuccessful farm people—his imagination had never really accepted them as his parents at all. The truth was that Jay Gatsby of West Egg, Long Island, sprang from his Platonic conception of himself. He was a son of God—a phrase which, if it means anything, means just that—and he must be about His Father's business, the service of a vast, vulgar, and meretricious beauty. So he invented just the sort of Jay Gatsby that a seventeen-year-old boy would be likely to invent, and to this conception he was faithful to the end. (98)

How does this passage represent Gatsby's belief in changing oneself (and one's past) in order to change one's destiny?

The Great Gatsby Overview: Meaning & Inferences 1 Page 3

5. Refer to the passage below:

> But he knew that he was in Daisy's house by a colossal accident. However glorious might be his future as Jay Gatsby, he was at present a penniless young man without a past, and at any moment the invisible cloak of his uniform might slip from his shoulders. So he made the most of his time. He took what he could get, ravenously and unscrupulously— eventually he took Daisy one still October night, took her because he had no real right to touch her hand.
>
> He might have despised himself, for he had certainly taken her under false pretenses. I don't mean that he had traded on his phantom millions, but he had deliberately given Daisy a sense of security; he let her believe that he was a person from much the same stratum as herself—that he was fully able to take care of her. As a matter of fact, he had no such facilities—he had no comfortable family standing behind him, and he was liable at the whim of an impersonal government to be blown anywhere about the world.

Does Gatsby feel the need to take Daisy as a possession? Explain what this reveals about Gatsby or Daisy.

The Great Gatsby Overview: Meaning & Inferences 2

Read the passage and answer the related questions.

On the last night, with my trunk packed and my car sold to the grocer, I went over and looked at that huge incoherent failure of a house once more. On the white steps an obscene word, scrawled by some boy with a piece of brick, stood out clearly in the moonlight, and I erased it, drawing my shoe raspingly along the stone. Then I wandered down to the beach and sprawled out on the sand.

Most of the big shore places were closed now and there were hardly any lights except the shadowy, moving glow of a ferryboat across the Sound. And as the moon rose higher the inessential houses began to melt away until gradually I became aware of the old island here that flowered once for Dutch sailors' eyes — a fresh, green breast of the new world. Its vanished trees, the trees that had made way for Gatsby's house, had once pandered in whispers to the last and greatest of all human dreams; for a transitory enchanted moment man must have held his breath in the presence of this continent, compelled into an aesthetic contemplation he neither understood nor desired, face to face for the last time in history with something commensurate to his capacity for wonder.

And as I sat there brooding on the old, unknown world, I thought of Gatsby's wonder when he first picked out the green light at the end of Daisy's dock. He had come a long way to this blue lawn, and his dream must have seemed so close that he could hardly fail to grasp it. He did not know that it was already behind him, somewhere back in that vast obscurity beyond the city, where the dark fields of the republic rolled on under the night.
Gatsby believed in the green light, the orgastic future that year by year recedes before us. It eluded us then, but that's no matter — to-morrow we will run faster, stretch out our arms farther. . . . And one fine morning ——

So we beat on, boats against the current, borne back ceaselessly into the past.

1. Why is the beach a significant setting?

2. What are "the last and greatest of all human dreams"?

The Great Gatsby Overview: Meaning & Inferences 2 Page 2

3. How is Gatsby's "wonder" different than the explorers' "wonder"?

4. What does the green light symbolize?

5. What is the significance of how the final sentence of the second to last paragraph is punctuated?

The Great Gatsby Overview:
How Is The Great Gatsby A Tragedy And What's To Be Learned From It?

A "tragedy" can be defined as a literary work in which the "hero" or some great person suffers defeat or destruction caused by a flaw in character or some overriding power, such as fate or societal forces.

Consider that definition as it may apply to The Great Gatsby.
- Who is the "hero" who suffers defeat or destruction? Is there more than one?
- What causes that destruction? (There could be multiple causes.)
    - Character flaw(s)?
    - Involvement with others?
    - Others' character flaws?
    - Societal forces?
    - Fate?

After you determine the cause of the hero's destruction, think about the story as a whole and determine what lessons we can learn from it.

Part I:
Which character(s) suffer defeat and/or destruction in The Great Gatsby? State the character's name, how that character was destroyed or defeated, and the page number in the text where that destruction is evidenced.

Character	What Happened?	Page Ref.

The Great Gatsby Overview:
How Is The Great Gatsby A Tragedy, And What's To Be Learned From It? Page 2

Part II

Use this chart (and additional pages, if needed) to collect, analyze and evaluate information. Put your line items from the What Happened column on the chart on the previous page in the What Happened column below. Working left to right, trace back the causes of the events to their roots.

What Happened?	Immediate Cause	What Caused The Immediate Cause?	What Caused That? What Is The Root Cause, The Root of the Problem?

The Great Gatsby Overview:
How Is The Great Gatsby A Tragedy, And What's To Be Learned From It? Page 3

Part III

Look at the Root Causes column on the chart you completed on the previous page. Review the kinds of things that are there. They could be things like greed, pride, desires for social standing, selfishness, loneliness, or many others.

Consider these things and the effects they have had on the characters in the book. Look at how the characters have interacted with each other. Think about these things in context of the themes and other elements you have discussed in class, then come up with a list of things readers could/should learn from reading The Great Gatsby. Next to each item on your list, write a few sentences explaining what elements in the book brought you to that conclusion. Continue on additional pages if necessary.

Things To Be Learned From The Great *Gatsby*	Elements In The Book That Support This Conclusion

The Great Gatsby Overview:
How Is The Great Gatsby A Tragedy, And What's To Be Learned From It? Page 4

Extra Page For Notes or Additional Information from Part I, II, or III

The Great Gatsby Overview: Creative Analytical Writing Assignments

1. Imagine Gatsby wrote a plan for his life. Write a paragraph describing his plans to throw parties that would attract Daisy.

2. Write a poem about living in the Valley of Ashes.

3. Write dialogue between Jordan and Daisy in the "present" of the novel in which Jordan asks Daisy about what happened the night before her wedding.

4. Write a magazine article that interviews Jordan Baker about being a modern woman and female athlete.

5. Write a letter from Nick to Gatsby's father that explains the enclosed book he wrote about Gatsby.

6. Rewrite the first page of the novel as a prologue, revisiting the issues and advice that Nick raises. Reflect Nick's life experiences and new perspectives in the prologue.

7. Imagine Nick writes an autobiography. Create an outline of the major events.

8. Nick imagines that the decade of his thirties stretching ahead of him will be lonely. Write an account of what you believe happens to him.

9. Select an omitted scene that is represented by ellipses in the novel. Write a version of the scene.

10. Imagine that T.J. Eckleburg is an omniscient presence. Describe what T.J. Eckleburg has witnessed.

The Great Gatsby Overview: Quick-Write Writing Assignments

1. In the 1920s, cars were beginning to have a major effect on American society for the first time. What does the car symbolize in the novel?

2. Which woman is more progressive, Daisy or Jordan? Why?

3. Nick and Gatsby are both veterans of World War I. The war was the first war with wide scale modern technologies and large, multiple fronts. The devastation caused by the war was beyond that which had ever happened previously. How does this character detail affect their relationship and make them different than other characters?

4. Which character is the most careless? Why?

5. Is Nick a reliable narrator? Explain.

6. How does Fitzgerald's use of ellipses/omissions affect the narrative?

7. Nick conveys information about Gatsby in chapter 6 out of the sequence that he receives it. Why is this significant? How does this relate to Nick's father's advice at the very beginning of the novel?

8. The novel is set during Prohibition, so all drinking of alcohol would be illegal. Why do people like Tom, Nick and Gatsby's party guests break the law?

9. Why does Nick feel compelled to tell Gatsby's story?

10. What is the significance of making Gatsby a criminal? Does it affect characters' sympathy for him?

www.ingramcontent.com/pod-product-compliance
Lightning Source LLC
Chambersburg PA
CBHW081458070526
44586CB00019B/2417